MERRIE WAKEFIELD

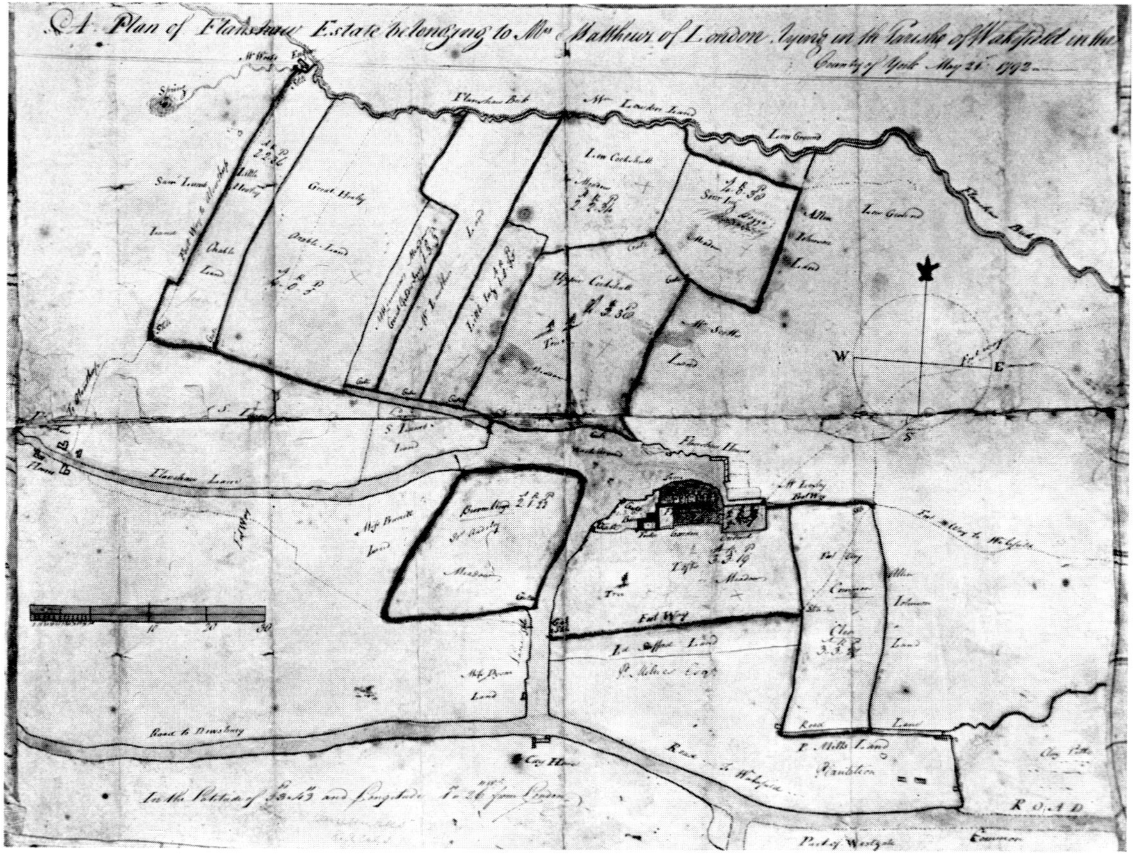

Survey map of Flanshaw Estate made in 1792

MERRIE WAKEFIELD

(based on some of the Diaries of Clara Clarkson (1811-89)
of Alverthorpe Hall, Wakefield)

by

ANN K. JACQUES

Printed and published by
THE WEST YORKSHIRE PRINTING CO. LTD., WAKEFIELD
1971

Contents

		page
	Introduction	ix
Chapter 1	Early Wakefield	1
2	Reform	8
3	Dinner at Four	15
4	Cholera	25
5	A Visit to Sheffield	29
6	Slavery	35
7	The Wakefield Soke	42
8	Local Affairs and Lead Coffins	47
9	Steel Pens and Influenza	53
10	Toll Bars and the Letters of Junius	62
11	Historic Place Names	71
12	Sunday School Affairs	76
13	Storms, Prayers when Salting Pork	82
14	Enter Victoria	87
15	Elections and Riots, Anti-Cruelty Society	97
16	Harrogate – Bone Houses	107
17	Sin-Eating – More Storms and Floods	118
18	Mr. Cameron Preaches Social Reform	124
19	Temperance, Drink and Drains	130
20	The Years Between	135
21	Convalescence	138
22	Bulls and Bears, Courts Baron	144
23	Income Tax 2d. in the Pound – Trouble in Salt-Pie Alley	152
24	Getting a Will Signed and Investments Arranged	158
25	Typhoid Outbreak – 'Rights for Women' and Rain Water	165

List of Illustrations

	page
Survey map of Flanshaw Estate	Frontispiece
Alverthorpe Hall	facing 2
Playford Hall	,, 4
The Chantry Chapel	,, 20
Conisbro' Castle	,, 38
Black Profile of 'dearest mother'	,, 50
Westgate	,, 52
C. of E. Marriage Lines	,, 68
Northgate	,, 90
Wood Street	,, 94
Kirkgate, below the Church steps	,, 100
Wakefield Market Place	,, 116

Photography by Bruce Watt (Palmerston North, N.Z.)

In view of their number and length, the relevant notes have been placed at the end of each chapter rather than at the foot of each page.

Introduction

CLARA Clarkson, my great great aunt was born at Alverthorpe Hall, Wakefield in 1811. When she was 15 years old she began to keep a diary. She never used the word 'diary' herself, referring always to it as her 'journal' in which she recorded daily and sometimes thrice daily all that made up her quiet life, commenting on family affairs (often of families other than her own), on political and social happenings, on books and music, poetry and needle crafts and inevitably, on the weather, which seems to have been no truer to seasonal specification then than it is today. She kept up the diary habit throughout her long life and when she died there were 40 or more volumes, all of uniform size and bound in red or green morocco leather. They were written in cipher, a device calculated no doubt to discourage the prying eyes of servants and perhaps too, of Mama and Papa.

In her will the journals were left, with other benefits to Mary Clarkson, my great aunt. But the existence of Clara's Journals was no secret and the Trustees of her Estate were bombarded with letters from solicitors of families far and wide requesting that they be destroyed forthwith. After much deliberation, and where dates of specific events could be established, the journals covering those years were duly burned. Thus, Mary Clarkson acquired about half of the original number.

She broke the cipher and read them and considering many entries to be either unkind or indiscreet, she burned several more volumes.

When Mary Clarkson died, the residue of the journals came to my father and as long as I can remember, about ten red and green volumes sat on a top shelf of a bookcase and always I told myself that 'someday' I must read them, but when one is young 'someday' can be very far away, and I came to New Zealand in 1928 leaving them still unread. The next owner of the collection was my brother Michael. He remembered my interest in 'things past', so picking out four books at random he brought them to New Zealand for me in 1936. The rest he destroyed.

I was glad to own even a few of them, put them on the top shelf of a bookcase and there they stayed for another thirty years. In 1967, by an odd combination of circumstances 'someday' actually eventuated, and I took down the four volumes and began to read.

This sounds a simple enough task, but it was far from being so. The cipher was the least of the difficulties, – it was a very simple one, the vowels being left 'as is' and every other consonant being replaced by a numeral. The old English style of using what they called the long 's' for the first 's' wherever a double 's' occurred seemed to complicate the cipher. The writing is a closely written copperplate, done with a fine quill pen. The ink has faded to an anaemic pink, on paper yellowed with age. Mastering the technical difficulties of reading with the help of a flat Franklin magnifying glass I found the journal to be 'good in parts', rather like the proverbial curate's egg. Whilst fifty per cent could have no interest, then or now, to any one but the writer, the other fifty per cent has a genuine and general interest and a charm which could be, in part at least, the gift of the intervening years. It tells the story of a rather delicate girl, possessed of all the graces and accomplishments expected of young ladies of that era. She was, in fact, a perfect Jane Austen model. She was completely dominated by 'dearest mother' who brought her up to be very feminine but somewhat less than female. She was always carefully insulated from the dangers of an unsuitable marriage. She was a prim and pious girl, in no way remarkable except in the meticulous tenacity with which she recorded the details of her quiet life as she gradually evolved into a dreary, crusty old maid, entirely preoccupied by her gallstones and her God.

The interest in the journal lies not in my great great Aunt herself, but in her references to contemporary political and social events, and in the glimpses she gives of the modes and manners of those far off days – many of these references so brief and often so puzzling that it required very many hours of research in order to amplify and explain. Much of the journal is concerned with the routine of reading, card playing, calling and receiving callers, music, shopping and chapel going. Almost every sermon is noted and frequently evaluated. Much of this 'mixture as before – 3 times daily' has been omitted. A few names have been altered in order to avoid possible offence to descendants of families mentioned. The works of the following authors have been of great assistance in clarifying vague references and filling in missing bits of the historical jig-saw.

The Day Before Yesterday ..	J. W. Robertson Scott
English Social History	P. M. Trevelyan
Roads to Ruin	E. S. Turner
Short History of English Peoples ..	J. R. Green
The English Heritage	R. W. Finn
Dictionary of Phrase and Fable ..	Brewer
Memories of Merrie Wakefield ..	H. Clarkson
English Place Names	H. S. Stokes
Word Origins	J. T. Shipley
The Smallest Room	John Pudney
The English Saga	Arthur Bryant
British Anti-slavery Movement ..	R. Coupland
A History of Medicine	Douglas Guthrie M.D., F.R.C.S.

ANN K. JACQUES

Chapter 1

Early Wakefield

IN the year of 1811 the old King George III was quite blind and mad and his son, the Prince of Wales, was proclaimed regent – 'Prinny', who became George IV in 1820, was very little improvement on his father. He was neither blind nor mad but he was weak and foolish and fond of fat ladies. His saving grace lay in his encouragement of the arts and his popularising of the healthy joys of sea bathing. The uneasy strife with America which had persisted for many years was on the point of becoming a declared war. Ireland was in a fever of rebellion and misery. The rural population of England was rumbling with discontent due to the Corn Laws and the Enclosure Act, which made the rich richer and the poor poorer, so that the once contented and comfortable land worker, now hungry and dispossessed, drifted to the towns where housing was infinitely worse and food scarcer and dearer than ever. The overcrowded sordid conditions promoted petty crime and riots were commonplace in the large new industrial centres.

Wakefield was neither new nor industrial. It was a quiet little place, prosperous because it was a wool town. The woollen mills were on the outskirts; in the town itself stood the warehouses, the counting houses, the Cloth Hall, the Corn Exchange and the Cattle Market. The headquarters of the Aire and Calder Navigation Company were there and in pre-railway days inland waterways were the money spinners. There was a Court House and a prison, a lunatic asylum, a Cathedral, a theatre and a music salon and Assembly room where the upper crust of the Riding met for balls and banquets, lectures and concerts, lively events which gained for the county town of the West Riding of Yorkshire the title of 'Merrie Wakefield'.

London was not, in the days of the Georges, the social mecca it became in later Victorian days. The journey from the north was long, uncomfortable and even dangerous and young ladies 'came out' in their own county towns where life was gay and elegant for the well-to-do and where the poor lived mostly out of sight and mind, down dark alleys, yards and folds.

Much of my information about conditions and ways of life in old Wakefield is gained from the memoirs of Henry Clarkson, my great great uncle. He was born in 1801, published his memoirs in 1887 and lived to see the dawn of the 20th century. An old man looking back over the changing years comments on and explains many things which the day-to-day diarist takes for granted or etches in so lightly that after more than a hundred years the pictures seem rather dim.

It was in 1811 that the first steam boat was launched on the Clyde and although England was at war with France, Napoleon's Grand Army was preparing for its march into Russia, warmly clad in greatcoats of English cloth and stout boots made in Nottingham.

Henry Clarkson, describing the first scheduled 'flight' which took place in Wakefield in 1811, wrote 'A man "flew" from the battlements of the Parish Church onto the bowling green in Southgate – this flight was achieved by means of a rope with board attachment which left the "airman" free to simulate wings with his arms. His safe landing was watched by a breathless and delighted crowd'. In other parts of England similar displays were given, but not by the same 'airman', for not infrequently a painted white cross on wall or path marked for long after the 'spot where the body lay'. He tells of the Wakefield cattle market, which was the biggest in the West Riding, and where the Lord of the Manor (then the Duke of Leeds) took toll of every head of cattle offered for sale – note, NOT 'sold' but offered for sale. The 'Lord's

Alverthorpe Hall in the early years of this century – now demolished.

men' gathered the toll money as the cattle were driven into town by one of the four main roads. It was the delight of small boys to aid the 'lordsmen' to circumvent evaders.

The hub of the town was, and still is, the Bullring: In 1811 bull and bear baitings were held there, but bull baiting was declining in popularity. The last of the bull baitings around Wakefield district took place at Alverthorpe in 1821 but bear baiting went on till a much later date. Floggings were considered good public entertainment, the 'Cat' being administered for very minor offences. The last public flogging in Wakefield took place in 1814. Henry Clarkson wrote, 'The floggings generally began at 12 o'clock and our benevolent school-masters, by way of improving our morality, used to let us out of school a quarter of an hour earlier. The wretched culprit was tied with outstretched arms to the back of a cart which was drawn at a tolerable foot's pace, from Bailiff House to the Elephant and Castle in Westgate. The "Cat" was a formidable weapon, having strips of whip-cord about two feet in length with a knot in each string at intervals of two inches'. He goes on to relate 'the last flogging I can recall was that of a man convicted of stealing a few fowls from Alverthorpe Hall. On driving into the Inn yard the gates were shut and the man's back washed with gunpowder and water – the pain of this operation was almost greater than that endured in the flogging. The purpose of the treatment was to leave indelible marks on the man's back for the rest of his life.' The stocks or pillory was a less brutal punishment and also took place at noon, so that the public might have fun pelting the captive with bad eggs and other disgusting missiles. The punishment was inflicted for slander or bad language. Henry Clarkson wrote 'I can remember being held up in the arms of a servant, to look over the heads of the crowd at a man and a woman being so treated, and the strange sight made an impression on me which I have never forgotten'.

Law and Order in the town were in the hands of the Chief Constable, an elected dignitary but a noticeable recurrence of certain family names in the record of office holders might give rise to a suspicion that the accident of birth had just a little to do with the election. The word 'constable' is one of the words which has come down in the world with the passage of time. It was derived from the Teutonic title of 'Count of the stable', the English equivalent of 'Master of the King's horse', and a Constable was a person of some consequence. The down-to-earth tasks of keeping order in the town were left to a few old men – twelve night-watchmen, in fact, who patrolled the streets from dusk to dawn and between rounds sheltered, and often slept, in watch boxes, before which burned tall tripod braziers on cold winter nights. These night-watchmen were generally referred to as 'Charlies' because it was in the time of Charles I that they had been reorganised and their employment promoted. To be likened to a 'Charlie' was never really regarded as a compliment. There was little street lighting; in the winter months a few oil lamps were affixed to brackets on suitable buildings, but the light was so feeble that a person standing by one lamp had difficulties in espying a glimmer from the next lamp ahead. During the summer months even these few lights were removed and stored till winter came again. Anyone venturing from home after dusk invariably carried a lantern.

The streets were narrow and unsurfaced and, in wet weather, became so muddy and soggy that wheeled vehicles often sank up to their axles and were immobilised. There was a raised cobbled causeway for pedestrians, and between this walk and the highway ran an open drain – agitators who wished for the closing of these drains were assured that closed drains bred fevers. The drains emptied into the river, which also provided the town's water supply.

These were the days of the Merchant Princes, who lived in a style more lavish and sophisticated than that of the old nobility. Dr. Johnson described them as 'a new species of gentlemen'. These new-rich were as keen as the old gentry on sport of all kinds. The local hunt met three times a week and the hounds were lodged in town at the houses of the members of the Hunt. The huntsman would ride through

Playford Hall, home of Thomas Clarkson, showing bricked-in windows – a means of reducing the window tax.

the Wakefield streets in his scarlet coat and black velvet cap and as he sounded his horn, the hounds would answer from all points of the compass and hasten to 'fall in', followed by every other dog in the town and so they would pass over Westgate Bridge to the appointed place for the Meet. Then these 'sportsmen' would release a 'bagged' fox, and the dazed and bewildered creature was hunted over unfamiliar terrain and no doubt a 'good time was had by all', except poor Reynard.

There were some very odd taxes to be paid in those days – most of them having been imposed by the greediest of kings, George III – salt and soap were taxed, silver, glass, clocks, watches, windows and periwigs. The taxes were collected by itinerant excise-men, a class noticeably accident-prone, particularly, it is said, when visiting glass factories. The glass tax (1745 to 1845) was imposed, not on the finished article, but 'at the furnace mouth', that means, when the metal was in the melting pot, prior to manufacture. This tax was at the rate of 1d. per lb. and made no allowance for breakages during processing, or marketing, and as much transport was by pack-horse or by ill-sprung waggons on bumpy roads, the breakages were a considerable factor. 'Black market' glass came into being at this time, particularly in Scotland. The goods were sold by hawkers who carried their packs on their backs and were too numerous and elusive for any check to be kept. A type of 'shoddy' glass was also made to circumvent taxation and was made by melting down old broken glass and remolding it – a cheap and nasty production.

The window tax was an iniquity, as it deprived people of light and air. A brick removed from an outer wall to admit ventilation counted as a window, a house with 6 windows paid 4s. a year and the rate per window increased with every extra window. My great great grandfather paid a window tax of seventeen pounds five shillings and it was not an immense house by any means. Windows larger than average were counted as two. The powder and periwig tax was a flat guinea a year and soon killed the fashion and so defeated its own purpose. My great great grandfather was, it seems, an obstinate man who wore his hair powdered and pigtail beribboned till his death in 1845; he and a Mr. Andrew Patersen were spoken of in Wakefield as 'the last of the guineapigs'.

These too, were the days of mantraps, spring guns and dog spears, of these the spring gun was most lethal, but the trap was a vile and crippling device. They were legal usage under the existing Game Laws, whereby only eldest sons of squires and persons of higher rank were allowed to shoot game. The use of spring guns was, in 1825 declared 'undesirable' unless used within a walled garden. Ten foot walls of dressed stone were built around stately homes and even enclosed vast park lands. A favoured topping to such walls consisted of broken glass set in cement. My great great grandfather was one of the first landowners in that part of Yorkshire to abandon the use of traps and guns. However, as a deterrent, he had notices placed in prominent places saying 'traps and guns set within these grounds' and had large painted posters erected depicting a poor wretch caught by the leg in a mantrap. The law against these hideous devices was not enacted until 1861 when it was eventually incorporated in the 'Offences against Persons Act' of that year.

Chimneys were swept by little boys, usually aged from 7 to 10 years. Proposed Acts abolishing such a practice were repeatedly thrown out in Parliament, but in 1834 it was made illegal for a boy under the age of 10 years to be apprenticed to a master sweep. In 1840 the age was raised to 16. This, it was hoped, would be tantamount to abolishing the practice, as most boys were too big at that age to climb an average chimney. Unfortunately the law was circumvented by using non-apprenticed boys and even, at times, by employing little girls. It was not until 1875 that the Earl of Shaftsbury piloted a Bill through the Lords which finally ended the malpractice.

The regency beaux carried vinaigrettes and pomanders and ladies were lavish with perfumes and sachets of potpourie. We are generally inclined to think of Regency days as an age of elegance, and so it may well have been at certain levels, but at the lowest levels it was an age of cruelty and squalor and at all levels it was rather smelly and far from healthy.

Chapter 2

Reform

1831

CLARA began writing her journal in 1826, but the records of the first five years are amongst the missing, no doubt destroyed 'by request'. The oldest volume in my possession is dated on the first page 1831 Sunday October 9th, and it reads 'We went to chapel in the morning and again in the afternoon. In the evening my Uncle Wood and William called to tell us that the Reform Bill[1] had been thrown out by the Lords. When they went I read the New Testament in French'.

October 10th. I studied French grammar in the morning and think it very dry. In the afternoon Eb called. It was a very rainy day, so Mother and Alfred and Eb and I played at Quadrille, and afterwards Eb and Alfred sang duets and I accompanied them on the piano.

October 12th. Learning French grammar in the morning. In the afternoon my Grandmother called and Sarah and Hannah Lindley and my Aunt Wood and Jane. Sarah is very much changed, she is very fat and looks so grown up and prim. Hannah puts me quite out of patience. She is only 14 and is the most self-confident and forward girl I ever saw. She joined in the conversation with my Mother and my Aunt and talked upon every subject like a woman of twenty-five. She asked me to go to drink tea with them one day next week.

October 13th. I relined my straw bonnet with satin and trimmed it with a velvet ribbon, then I finished knitting the stockings for Alfred. In the afternoon Elizabeth Asquith called and I showed her how to do netting for a cap.

October 15th. Eb called with a Miss Colbeck from Leeds, and Captain Dawson and John called to ask us to take tea with them next Wednesday and then the two Miss Hausleys called. I like the elder one much better than Mary Ann.

October 16th. We went to Chapel and my Grandmother and John came home with us, and after dinner we went again to Chapel.

October 17th. My Uncle and Aunt Wood called and they and Mother and I played a very long pool of Quadrille. My Aunt was in one of her best humours and we were very agreeable indeed.

October 18th. Alfred and I called for Cousin Ann and we went to Flanshaw to visit my Grandmother. Elizabeth, Hannah and Samuel Lindley were there and Sarah Heald. They were talking about Thomas S. who has forgotten all about poor Miss M. and is paying much attention to Miss H. Sarah talked of her beaux as if she were quite grown up. Alfred and Samuel talked of their Philosophical Society most of the time. We stayed till half past seven and were most agreeable, but I had a headache and did nothing but think of what Mother would say to our staying so long. It really was not my place to say anything about going home, but at last I was obliged to do so as I felt so uneasy. We all left together. Mother did not actually say anything but she seemed to be offended.

October 19th. Mother and Alfred and I went to Alverthorpe Hall. All the family were there, the 'Rev.' Henry too. At first they talked about the Gaskells. Today is Milnes Gaskell's twenty-first birthday and they had 150 trades people of Wakefield to dine and 600 poor people of Thornes and Alverthorpe dined in the open-air. There is to be a ball tonight and fireworks. Captain Dawson says 'what fools they are'. The 'Rev.' Henry talked of Harrogate. He says that Mother goes there for her health and that I go to find a beau. He says I should persuade her to go to Burlington[2] or Scarbro', where I should be sure to find a sweetheart. I was quite provoked by him but only gave him a look of contempt. The creature calls me 'Clara' without having asked if he may. It was not easy to keep my temper. He said nasty things too about the 'Jocinian' religion as he always calls the Unitarians. He says it is just a religion for genteel people, and no good for the poor. I am afraid he has no real religion in him at all. His father and John and Mrs. Henry did not say very much. We came away at half past six and I wished we had never gone. It is never a happy house for me.

October 20th. Eb called and she told me that her father and mother had been at the ball at Thornes House last night. When she went Mother was much worse about dear Eb than ever before. She seems quite cross whenever I mention her name or any of her family, and I can't tell why. What can I do? Dear Eb and I are just like sisters and I know she loves me better than any of my other companions. I feel so grieved. I cried famously about it in bed when Mother could not know.

October 23rd. I felt ill so Mother and Alfred went to Chapel and I stayed home and read the Book of Job. In the afternoon I felt better and went to Chapel. Cousin Ann walked home with me and stayed to drink tea.

October 25th. Alfred went to the theatre with William Johnstone to see Mr. Matherson perform. Mother and I sat up for him and played draughts. Alfred did not come home till after 12 o'clock.

October 26th. My cousin Lawrance came to breakfast. He brought a letter from my cousin Benjamin. It is years since we saw Lawrance before. In the evening Alfred went to a meeting of his Philosophical Society and did not get home till after eleven. Mother and I played draughts again.

October 28th. Called at my Uncle Wood's. Jane had just returned from Harrogate and she told me that she had walked ALONE with a young man in the fields whilst she was there. Captain Dawson is quite right, – there is nothing these girls will not do to acquire a beau. She also told me that Miss C. had told her that her brother was

Eb's lover[3] and that Miss C. had said that she would be quite delighted to have Eb as a sister.

November 10th. Miss Williamson is here to make me a blue stuff frock with a pelerine and I helped her in the morning. In the evening Mother and I went to a party at the Clapham's. There were many guests, and my cousin the 'Rev.'[4] Thomas Clarkson was there. He came and sat by me and said 'Well Clara, I do declare you have grown into a great girl since I last saw you'. I know I should have had a kiss had we been in a less public place, and I was very glad indeed to escape it. My cousin Ann picked up a pack of cards and asked him if he tolerated such things. He said 'Oh yes, but I never play myself'. Some of us played whist in the upstairs drawing room, and later we joined the others downstairs and danced quadrilles. I played for them most of the time. Mr. C. asked me to leave the piano and dance with him but Mother thought we should be going home. Charles Clapham asked to be allowed to see us home but Mother explained that a servant was waiting to accompany us. It had really been a most pleasant evening.

November 11th. Captain Dawson and John called. They really are becoming tiresome, always wanting Mother to do things for them, things which she thinks they should do for themselves. Miss Williamson is here again, making Mother a frock and I helped her. She is making me another frock and relining my cloth cloak and adding a full cape. I am so sorry for Miss Williamson; she had a lover for 5 years and now he has gone off and married someone else. Mother and I went into town and changed our books at the library and called to tell K. to go to Alverthorpe to mend the pump which the Dawsons have been complaining about.

November 16th. The people who live opposite to the Burtons are in a sad state. Mrs. Thomas Turner who was confined a few days ago has a brain fever, and not expected to recover. She is a very pretty woman and only 18 years old. Eb went across to see her and she says that Thomas is quite distraught. Mother and I went into town and on our way home called at B.'s and ordered half a pig.

November 18th. Our new piano arrived today and I am delighted with it. It is a great improvement on the old one, it has more keys and an extra pedal and everyone admires the tone. The new tenant at Hardwick (Mr. Jessop) dined with us and he is very musical, he would have had me play all day. Later, dear Eb and her mother called and cousin Jane and Mary Ann and we played and sang interminably. Poor Jane had stumbled as she came along the lane and her cloak was covered in mud. Hannah took it and cleaned it for her.

December 1st. I am now giving piano lessons to Alfred each morning. He has a nice singing voice and I am sure he will soon be good on the piano. Mother is trying to arrange for him to go as a pupil to a Mr. Walker, who is a surveyor and Commissioner of Crown Lands.

December 2nd. News came today that Harriet Ellerby (nee Clarkson) was killed a few days ago. She was thrown from a gig in which she was riding at Richmond and died later of concussion. It has been a great shock, they were married quite recently. Oh God, how inscrutable are Thy ways, teach us to be prepared and ready whenever Thou deemest best to summon us. Amen.

December 18th. Mother and Alfred went to Chapel but I felt so ill I stayed at home and read extracts from a book of sermons and then 'Elegent Epistles'. I have been feeling so ill lately and I really fancy it is all caused by worms. Recently they have been getting worse, and I have been most uneasy about it. They torment me every day.

December 20th. The old clothes woman came today and I sold her three frocks for five shillings.

December 23rd. It is all arranged for Alfred to go to Mr. Walker's as a pupil and mother is to pay him one-hundred pounds a year for 3 years. Elizabeth Asquith called; she and Alfred and I played three handed whist.

December 25th. Sunday and Christmas Day. Mr. Cannon preached a beautiful sermon. He is a bachelor and now almost all the young ladies in the parish are in love with him. After Chapel my Aunt and Uncle Wood and seven cousins and Uncle John came to dine with us and their servants joined Hannah in the kitchen so there were two dinner parties in the house. After dinner we played the piano and everyone sang gloriously. Then we danced several sets of Quadrilles and the cousins lectured Alfred about his unfashionable dress and they urged him to wear a surtout and to have his hair curled, and vowed they would teach him to dance. Then we dressed him up in a cloak of Mother's and one of my bonnets and he went out and came and knocked at the door. Hannah admitted him without recognising him and Mother thought he was Mrs. H. from Flanshaw Lane, but at last he laughed and disclosed himself. They all went away at about 9 o'clock and we had been most agreeable and merry. When they had gone, Mother told Hannah to bring her brother to look at the new piano. He is a flautist and quite a judge in musical matters. I played several short pieces of music for him and he looked very shy and stood at a respectful distance.

December 29th. We dined at my Uncle Wood's. Grandmother, John and Amy were there and William and Margaret Johnstone. My cousins and I discussed the propriety of taking singing lessons from Miss Scarth and agreed to do so if her terms were suitable. We then joined the others and played whist. Sometimes I grow very weary of playing cards always.

[1] Mention of the Parliamentary Reform Bill on the first page seemed most promising. What I knew of the matter might not have fitted on a postage stamp, but it could have been written comfortably on the back of an envelope, so it seemed advisable to do a little historical research in order to fill in the background to any further contemporary comment. The Parliamentary Reform Movement had been going on for sixty years or more. In 1869 a Mr. John Wilkes, Member of Parliament for Middlesex, was expelled from the House of Commons for having dared to criticise the Address from the Throne. This act of expulsion set the spark to the fuse of a bloodless revolution. Middlesex was angered by such treatment of their elected member. Wilkes was made an Alderman, and the Lord Mayor, Aldermen and Livery of London petitioned King George III to dissolve a Parliament which, they declared, no longer represented the people. The King rejected their petition and Parliament issued a decree prohibiting the publication of its debates and proceedings and the Lord Mayor of London was sent to the Tower. The people of Middlesex were

roused. They loudly supported the Lord Mayor and Mr. Wilkes, and resented the suppression of a free press. There were many ugly and bitter scenes in the London streets. The King and his Ministers could read the writing on the wall. They quietly dropped their charges against the people's representatives, and withdrew the decree forbidding publication of debates. After this time a great English free press emerged as the mouthpiece of the people of England; the Chronicle, the Morning Post and the Times all developed in the ensuing years, giving the people news and views in a responsible manner not previously enjoyed. It is true that a vast number of the population were unable to read, but they were not deaf even if they were illiterate. Lecturers toured the length and breadth of the land and meetings were held at which the new doctrines of Liberty, Equality and Fraternity were preached and public opinion was organised as never before. By the time that William IV came to the throne these new teachings were beginning to bear fruit. At first, William tried to follow the pattern set by his predecessors, and seemed to hold some lingering belief in the Divine Right of Kings, a doctrine which the people no longer accepted. When the Reform Bill was thrown out by the King and the Lords on October 7th 1831, a wave of resentment swept the country and Earl Grey and his ministers resigned in protest. This news, which Clara reports in her journal on Sunday October 9th had taken the best part of three days to travel north. There was a postal service at that time but it was geared to horse-power in a very literal sense. The quiet reception of the delayed news on Sunday evening in Wakefield was very different from the reaction to it in the south and Midlands. On that Sunday morning the carriages of the wealthy churchgoers were stoned by the mobs in London's fashionable streets, for it was well noted that the Lord Bishops had been prominent amongst the Bill's rejectors. The Bishops had voted 22 against and only 3 for the motion. It is said that the number of fires which occurred in the palaces of Bishops and in churches during the next few months were far from being coincidental. Though there seemed to be very little immediate reaction in Wakefield, there was a real and growing resentment against delayed reform. No reference occurs in the journal to political affairs for some 6 months and meanwhile Clara busily records the happenings in her own small world.

[2] Now called Bridlington.

[3] The word 'lover' had not at that time acquired the questionable implication which it has today.

[4] The prefix 'Rev.' is underlined, and seems to have been a constant source of vexation to Clara for Unitarian and other non-conformist ministers were not at that time accorded the civility which was reserved for the clergy of the established church.

Chapter 3

Dinner at Four

1832

JANUARY 2nd. Alfred went for the first time to Mr. Walker's office. The other pupils are William Johnstone, Thomas Nicholson and a Mr. Day, all fine fashionable young men. I do hope they will behave well to Alfred who seems so different from them. Poor Hannah's sister has just died in child-bed and Hannah is going into black. I am making a mourning cap for her.

January 4th. We had a very keen frost last night and are very pleased. The streets have been so dirty lately that we have not been able to go out. Now we can walk on the hard ground. Mother and I went shopping and mother bought a black cloth shawl for Hannah. On the way home we called at my Uncle John's and found Mary very ill again. She laughs and talks to herself all the time and is in a high fever. Mrs. Henry Clarkson was there. She says that Mary is in a very dangerous state. She walked home with us part of the way and we thought she looked ill, and she is, I fancy, enceinte.

January 12th. Mother and I went to my Uncle Wood's. They were having a large children's party, the little Barffs, Micklethwaites, Marriotts, Holdsworths, Hardcastles and the two Shaw children. Miss Bell came with the Charlesworths. She is about eighteen and is just coming out. A very nice girl. My cousin Ann and I played alternately for the children's games and dancing. They had a cold supper, simple, but it all looked very nice. It was all very pleasant; I love to see the children dancing. As we came home the road was so muddy I feared I should stick fast in it. Mother had taken pattens and so was better off, and she kept encouraging me but it was a sad end to the lovely party.

January 14th. Mr. Walker called with one of his clerks and Alfred signed his indentures and Mother paid Mr. Walker a hundred pounds. In the afternoon Mr. Walker had a dinner party for his pupils and their friends. I had been asked but declined. They dined at 4 o'clock. As they were leaving the dinner table shortly after 9 o'clock[1] Alfred slipped away. The others joined the ladies for dancing but Alfred is not dancing just yet.

January 27th. Mother had received a summons to attend at the Court House on account of a Parish orphan whom they wish her to take. But she has a cold and did not go out, so she sent for Mr. G., one of the Court House Overseers, and agreed to pay ten pounds instead, so it was settled. Alfred told us that John Burton has bought four-hundred pounds worth of wool from Michael Tunnicliffe and about three-hundred pounds worth from Mr. Gotthurst and from some other people, including his brother Henry, and that he has cheated them and gone off with the money. I am sorry to hear this, for dear Eb's sake. She seems to have trouble after trouble.

February 1st. Today I felt well enough to call on dear Eb. It is quite true about John, just as Alfred told us. She knows very little more than we were told, except that he has with him a portrait painter called Dobbins, and it is supposed that they have taken shipping at Liverpool for New York. John has taken more than three-thousand pounds of other people's money. Michael Tunnicliffe followed them as far as Liverpool, but the ship he believes they were on had sailed. I persuaded dear Eb to come home with me, which she did, and stayed till 8 o'clock and then Alfred took her home.

February 6th. Copied music of some psalms which cousin Jane had lent me then I began making another night-shirt for Alfred. In the afternoon I went shopping with mother and we got a bottle of Macassar oil and went to Kirkbrides about our new bonnets. We called at my uncle John's on the way home and found Mary a little better.

February 8th. Went to call on the Burtons and found Eb very ill, numb, fainting and cold all over. We persuaded them to send for Mr. Bennett, the surgeon, and Mr. Burton went for him.

February 12th. Went to Chapel and Mr. Cannon preached the best sermon I have ever heard on the text 'Who art thou that judgeth another?' We went again in the afternoon and he preached again, a sort of appendix to his morning sermon.

February 13th. Dear Eb is very ill. Dr. Bennett says it is a nervous complaint caused by John's behaviour. He told Eb she must go out and mix with people as much as possible and try not to think of John. As we walked home we met several people who spoke of the affair and said the Burtons were disgraced for ever, and they seemed to almost exult in their misfortunes. I was provoked almost beyond endurance.

February 16th. Captain Dawson and John called. They want Mother to lower their rent. I finished a nightshirt for Alfred, then Jane Wood called and we went together to look at the estate in Westgate which used to belong to Rushworths, the Bankers,[2] who failed a little time ago, and her uncle Barff has now bought it. The house is large and elegant and there are hot houses and a summer house and beautifully laid out gardens. On our way home we bought silk stockings. My cousins are going to a dance at the Hardcastle's tomorrow.

February 17th. Today is my 21st birthday. Oh God Almighty, if it be Thy Blessed will to spare me for another year, grant that I may be more worthy to receive Thy mercies and more prepared to meet my dying hour. Amen.

February 19th. I felt too ill to go to Chapel. My Aunt and Uncle Wood went with Mother and Alfred, expecting that Mr. Johnstone would preach the funeral sermon for Mr. Marriott, but he did not. At the Old Church there was a funeral sermon for the Rev. Thomas Rogers and the church was more crowded than it has been for many a day.

February 24th. Mr. and Mrs. Scatcherd and Samuel came to dine with us and then we all went into town to see a wax-works show. There were 200 wax figures but after the fine advertisement in the newspaper we were very disappointed. It had stated that there would be a 'handsome promenade constructed for the company and seats provided for the nobility'. It was quite laughable to see the actual shabbyness of it all. The figures were well enough dressed, all characters from ancient history, but the light from the high windows shone directly on to them making them difficult to see. They would have looked much better by candle light. We returned home to drink tea and Mr. Scatcherd told us all over again about the wonderful Cremonas[3] violin which had 'slipped through his fingers'. He admired the new piano, but managed to imply that it was vastly inferior to his own. They wanted me to return to Morley with them but I did not feel well enough.

March 3rd. Called at Mr. Burton's. William is just recovering from the measles. He and Henry and Eb and I played at Loo. Eb told me that they have no more news yet from John, but that he has been declared bankrupt and the creditors are going to sell his life interest in his mother's fortune[4] and poor Eb is much distressed.

March 5th. Mother and I went for quite a long walk and we called to tell Kettle (the gardener) to come tomorrow. In the evening Alfred went to the theatre to hear a political lecture by someone called Cotterell.

March 12th. Called at Eb's and played cards as usual. Eb told me that the creditors can do nothing and get nothing so long as Mrs. Burton lives, and that should John die before his mother, the money will be divided amongst the remaining members of the family. Eb is very delighted about this, but it does seem to be a little hard on the creditors.

March 14th. There is something about John Burton almost every week now in the newspaper, which is a little bit difficult for the family. I had my music bound and now I am backing the book with calico. Reading the 'History of New York'.

March 19th. My Uncle Wood called with his solicitor and I signed a parchment renouncing all further claim on my uncle's estate.

March 21st. Today is a General Fast Day on account of the Cholera. We all went to Chapel and Mr. Johnstone preached from 17th Chapter of Luke, verses 26 to 31.

April 5th. Eb called and she told me that they had had a letter from John who says he is well and safe and he enclosed some money for Eb and Henry. The creditors have heard about it and claim the money but Mrs. Burton will not give it up and Eb seems to think very little now of the wrong that John has done. She abused the creditors for wanting the money. I really was rather shocked and surprised to hear her say that the amount that John had taken was only a 'paltry sum'. Mr. Gotthurst (one of the creditors) had been talking to her and told her, that if John were found he could be transported. He does not believe that John is in America, but says he may be in Lisbon with George Croft with whom he was so friendly. I pity Eb very much but I think she is wrong to say some of the things she does, but then she is so very intelligent . . . I always think she is too intelligent for a woman.

April 9th. Went into town and got our library subscriptions renewed. In the afternoon Captain and John Dawson called, I felt very ill indeed and went to bed very early.

April 13th. Mrs. Benjamin called, she is visiting at New Millar Dam. My grandmother told me that she hoped to live long enough to see me happy with a good husband, and I asked her if she could not be content to see me happy without the husband?

April 15th. Mother did not go to Chapel as she has a bad cough. I went with Alfred but did not feel at all well. We called at my Uncle John's on the way home as there had been none of the family at Chapel. Henry has had a high quarrel with the Johnstones, – something about William, who was a pupil of Henry's but left him and went to Mr. Walker when Alfred did. I would not be at all surprised if Henry left our Chapel now.

April 20th. Mary Ann Housley married her cousin Samuel Housley today. He is a Merchant Tailor of London. He drove from London for the wedding in his own fine carriage and four horses, and Charles Housley told Alfred that he had brought 'a cart load of jewells' for Mary Ann.

April 23rd. Easter Sunday. Cousin Jane and I went to the Catholic Chapel this morning. We sat at the back of the gallery quite high up and watched them whilst they performed a Mass. The altar was decorated with flowers. A clergyman preached on the divinity of Christ . . . no doubt a most edifying sermon, but Jane and I both felt our time ill spent and determined never to go there again. Richard S. dined with us and quite confirmed us in our opinions.

April 24th. Mr. Walker of Westgate Common has been found drowned in the river. We saw them taking him home. Eb's brother Henry is engaged to his daughter Mary.

April 27th. Called for my cousin Mary Ann and we went together to call on Mrs. Johnstone. Mrs. Ledger called whilst we were there. She is much wishing to form a Literary Society for ladies who wish to improve their minds. She asked me and I said I thought it too ridiculous. It is so like Mrs. L., she just thinks of things to attract notice. She asked Ann and Miss Kendal to join but they would not. When she left we were very merry about it. Mary Ann and I then walked along to Flanshaw Hall to visit my grandmother.

May 6th. Mr. Cannon preached in the morning and Mr. Johnstone in the afternoon. Mother did not go to Chapel today as she has a cold. After supper one of my uncle's servants came to tell us that my grandmother had had an

The Chantry Chapel, from an engraving by T. Kilby in 1853. It was built in 1356-57 and the Battle of Wakefield was fought nearby in 1460.

accident and Uncle Wood had taken Mr. Benjamin Walker (the surgeon) with him to Flanshaw.

May 7th. We went to visit my grandmother and found that she has a broken shoulder and is in great pain. Mr. Walker took Mr. Naylor with him and set the shoulder and bound it up very tightly and he says she will have to keep it so for some time.

May 15th. Alfred's birthday. He is 19 years old today.

May 18th. Reading the newspaper. There is much writing and commotion about political matters lately. Earl Grey and his Ministers retired from office because of the Reform Bill being thrown out last October and the Duke of Wellington has been trying to form a government, but without success, so Earl Grey has been recalled, and is to be permitted to carry the Reform Bill without mutilation. There have been great rejoicings everywhere and a West Riding meeting is to be held in Wakefield next Wednesday to send an address to the King, to beseech him to put complete and un-deviating confidence in Earl Grey and his colleagues.

May 21st. Mother and I went to Morley. The weather was delightful but rather hot. We found them all well and full of news. In the evening I read 'The Life of Eugene Aron' written by Mr. Scatcherd.

May 22nd. We walked in the garden and talked a good deal and I helped Fanny to reline her bonnet. Later, we went to look at the new Sunday school which is being built. Several friends called to drink tea and later we had music and walked in the garden, for it was a delightfully warm evening.

May 23rd. We were awakened to the sound of music and of a great assemblage of people who were setting out for Wakefield. They all had orange ribbons in their hats and had orange flags, and were headed by Mr. Swinton. We set off for home in the gig, but when we got to Kirkhamgate we had to stop. The road was so crowded with people and carriages of all kinds from the highest to the lowest and we waited a while and then went on. As we neared Wakefield we heard all the church bells ringing and bands playing everywhere. We found Mr. Cassel waiting for us when we arrived home and after dining we all went with my uncle Wood to Mr. Barff's and sat with them in the summerhouse which overlooks the Ings and we had a wonderful view of the hustings. There were hundreds of flags flying and bands playing and it was computed that there were 200,000 people in Wakefield that day, and never was there such a multitude seen here before.

May 25th. We are much alarmed today to hear that the Cholera is in the town. They have taken a house near my uncle John's to use as a Cholera Hospital. One man has died of it. There is great talk of Mr. Johnstone preaching old sermons and they say that the congregation is growing smaller because of it.

May 31st. Mother and Mrs. Scatcherd and I went to see the display of fashions at Miss Naylor's but did not see anything we liked, then we went on to Miss Briggs' and saw some very nice things. Mrs. Scatcherd bought a cap and I bought a very pretty pelerine. Then we went to see about our new bonnets. As we came home we called at uncle John's but did not go in. Mary is very ill again. Mr. Burton called soon after we got home with a letter from dear Eb who is in Leeds. She told me that Mrs. Colbeck had a big party a few days ago and that they danced till 2 o'clock in the morning.

June 1st. Mrs. Scatcherd and Sarah Ann came to visit us.

June 3rd. Sunday. Mother and Mrs. Scatcherd, Sarah Ann and I went to Chapel in the morning and then to Thornes Church in the afternoon. Mr. Tyson read the prayers and Henry Dawson preached for quite half an hour and he could have said it all in ten minutes had he spoken in his usual manner. Mother and Mrs. Scatcherd then went to call on Mrs. H., but I went with Sarah Ann to my cousin Jane's and she did my hair up on top of my head and persuaded me to wear it that way in future.

June 7th. News came today that the Reform Bill had been passed. Mother and Mrs. Scatcherd and I went into town and I bought a high comb for my hair and gave five shillings for it. We called at my Uncle John's and found Mary much better though still in bed. They showed us some beautiful shawls which they bought recently and this pleased Mrs. Scatcherd who is so fond of dress.

June 17th. Sunday. Went to chapel with Alfred. Mother did not go as she has a bad cough. Mr. Johnstone preached a sermon which we had heard three or four times before. Elizabeth Asquith called with Miss Wetherell.

June 25th. Busy netting an edge for a frill for Mother. Miss Scarth (our singing teacher) came with her nephew who teaches dancing. He played the 'Harmonious Blacksmith' with variations and sang several songs in French and Italian. After they went, Mother and I called on my Uncle Wood and heard that the Cholera is again in Wakefield and everyone is very concerned about it.

[1] It seems that to spend four hours or even longer at table was not at all exceptional in those days. Four o'clock was the fashionable hour for dining, but 2 or 3 o'clock was quite usual *en famille*. Ladies retired from table somewhat earlier than is general today, or perhaps it would be more correct to say that the gentlemen remained at table after the ladies left them, longer than would be tolerated in our day. Whilst the port circulated, the ladies were served tea or coffee in the drawing room, and were joined later by such of the men folk as were in any condition to do so, and card playing, music or dancing was enjoyed. But in those days of heavy drinking it was not unusual for many men to be quite incapable of making the journey to the drawing room and many of them slept it off where they had dined.

Breakfast was rarely served before 10 o'clock, and was a sociable meal, friends frequently dropping in to join those at table, generally the younger members of the household, for it seems that breakfast in bed or in the bedroom was a rather general practice of the older generation. The period between 10 o'clock breakfast and dinner was called 'morning' and callers between those hours were offered wine with cake, fruit or bread and butter. Tea was served after dinner, usually around 5.30 and supper was an informal but often substantial snack around 9 o'clock. As the century aged, the hour for dining became later and later until at the end of the Victorian era it stabilised at about 8 o'clock. As dinner became a late day meal, tea was served earlier, but New Zealand seems to be the pioneer of tea at 3.30. Luncheon was not a scheduled meal in the early part of the century, but with earlier breakfast and later dinner it came into favour with its own special code of behaviour. Even in the very early years of this century it was a vulgarity for guests to sit down to luncheon hatless or gloveless. Ladies did not take cheese at this meal – or at dinner – as to be seen eating cheese would indicate an appetite more robust than genteel. On Sunday, meals were quite different and were arranged to be taken between church services, for most people attended Church or Chapel twice each Sunday and the mid-day meal was a great occasion for family gatherings and for meeting together of the pillars of the church, when sermons were discussed and subjected to the higher criticism and the fate of many a minister or curate was sealed at that time.

[2] The Bank to which Clara referred was the Private Bank of Wentworth, Challoner and Rushworth, which had branches in York, Wakefield and Huddersfield. In the years between 1825 and 1830 many private banks failed in England, and the cause was not what we today would term 'a recession' but rather the reverse. In ancient times men had kept their wealth in strongly guarded boxes, and later, when banks eventuated, they were regarded as safe places for accumulated wealth. But the Act of Enclosure and the Industrial Revolution had changed the picture. Money was now something which could be used to produce more money. People withdrew money from the banks to invest in the new factories and railways, and even in overseas ventures, and this run on gold caused many private banks to close their doors. Amongst these latter was the firm of Wentworth, Challoner and Rushworth. It was in the days before limited liability and the partners lost very heavily indeed, their private fortunes being forfeited to pay the creditors. Only such property as was entailed was saved from the ruin. The York branch, which had been managed by Challoner came off best, all the creditors being paid out in full. Huddersfield and Wakefield, managed by Wentworth and Rushworth respectively were less fortunate and of the three partners Rushworth fared the worst. The bank failure was a great blow to the district and it was a long time before confidence in the banking system was re-established. People had a tendency to hoard bank notes and gold.

[3] The Cremonas violins were, according to Brewer 'of the greatest excellence, so called from Cremona, where for many years lived some makers of violins who have gained a worldwide notoriety, such as Andrea Amati and his pupil Antonius Stradivarious'.

[4] The 'fortune' referred to here was no doubt a marriage settlement or dowry. As the law stood at that time, such monies were not the property of the wife. Prior to the year 1872, married women had no legal rights of ownership of monies or wealth of any kind. Even in the case of working women, the husband could legally possess himself of her hard earned wages. The Married Woman's Property Act corrected this unfair law. The phrase in the marriage service 'with all my worldly goods I thee endow' should really have been spoken by the bride, not by the bridegroom.

Chapter 4

Cholera

THE repeated references to Cholera in Clara's journal came as a surprise, for till then I had harboured the comfortable belief that such nasty diseases were disasters of dim and distant times. The Great Plague of London was in 1665 and most people know of it chiefly from the reading of Daniel Defoe and of Pepys' Diary. Defoe wrote as an eye witness though he was actually only six years old at that time, but his parents must have talked so often and so vividly about those bad days that he saw it all through their eyes.

Pepys was a grown man when it happened and he stayed at his post at the Admiralty when lesser men followed the king and the court to the provinces. But he records that he made his will and set his affairs in order 'lest it should please God to take him'. The Great Plague was followed by the Great Fire in 1666 and that cleaned up the filthy slum dwellings and a new and better city grew up on the ashes, and so 'all was for the best, in the best of all possible worlds', though those who dwelt in the squalor around Pudding Lane might have taken a less philosophical view of current affairs.

Plague, Black Death, Cholera are all names for one rather similar dread disease which has been the scourge of humanity since civilisation began, and civilisation began when man started to give up the nomadic life and settle in communities. The virulence of the disease fluctuated and details of its manifestation varied just as in our time the influenza scourge develops slightly different symptoms in each epidemic. The Plague is mentioned in the Bible. Douglas Guthrie in his History of Medicine wrote, 'it is believed that the emerods with which the Lord smote the

Philistines were the buboes of plague'. At that time it was believed that mice carried the disease and mice were frequently included in the ritual sacrifices. The Plague is mentioned in ancient Greek records and in those of early Roman and Egyptian times. The first recorded hospitals were built in Rome, to house those sick of the Plague, in 293 B.C.

Some suspicion must have been entertained as to the part played by rats in the spreading of the disease. In India, Greece and the Middle East snakes were venerated, just as cats were sacred in Egypt. Both snakes and cats were rat catchers. Most religious beliefs, ceremonials and practices have their roots originally in some practical and beneficial health regulation. Water too was suspect for a period, and Jews were held responsible and accused of poisoning the wells of Christians, so the Christians, full of pious indignation, burned many Jews at the stake. In the 17th century it was thought that dogs carried the disease and a fearful slaughter of dogs took place, even in England.

It is estimated that in 1348 the Black Death killed one quarter of the earth's population. Half the people in London died and at Avignon the Pope consecrated the river Rhone so that bodies might be cast into it and be considered to have received Christian burial. The Plague generally followed trade routes and in English ports, ships from the Levant were quarantined. Boccaccio relates that in 1353 people died in the streets and lay there unburied. Entire households perished and the whole town was filled with the stench of rotting bodies.

In medieval times people regarded disease as a visitation of God and a punishment for sin; the ugly red patches which developed on bodies just prior to death were called 'God's mark'.

In the late 18th and early 19th centuries blood-letting was resorted to, and vinegar was used as a mouth wash as a precautionary measure. But it was not until 1884 that a German physician, Robert Koch, established the fact that the infection was carried in drinking water and that the infection in the water was caused by human contamination aided considerably by the rat population – rats being susceptible to many human ailments. The flea seems to have had a clear charge sheet in respect to Cholera but in earlier types of plague it had been a very active carrier. Those who tended the sick or the dead incurred no greater risk than the rest of the community for the germs were water borne and had to be ingested orally. As one London medical man said, had all the pump handles been removed cholera would have departed with them. A bold assertion, but containing more truth than was generally conceded.

Slave ships brought the disease to the ports, particularly to Liverpool, Bristol, Glasgow and London. From 10% to 50% of the 'Black Cargo' usually died at sea in the 'middle passage' and were cast overboard.

In 1848 over 1,000,000 people died of Cholera in Europe and Glasgow had a particularly bad outbreak. When the North British railway was opened in October of 1849, all celebrations were cancelled because of the prevalence of Cholera.

The rat infestation in Europe must have been pretty general. In remote villages and in the great country houses, rats kept people awake at night. The account of the infestation of Hameln in the poem of 'The Pied Piper' was not over-drawn. Henry Clarkson, in his memoirs, records a visit to a lovely lakeland village in 1822 where the rats were so numerous that no traveller could sleep. He wrote that 'they chased each other up and down the bed hangings and across the bed itself and throwing things at them merely increased their acrobatic agility'. When action was taken against the rat menace it was not inspired by any consideration of hygiene but entirely on that of pounds, shillings and pence.

In the bad depression days of the Corn Law era the children of the poor were dying of malnutrition or growing up deformed and crippled. The workers were gaunt, hungry and morose, but the rats thrived and accounted for much loss of the precious grain. The Act of Enclosure passed in

1776 was being very gradually implemented but churches were still drawing tithes and the tithes were being robbed by the rats, so something had to be done. Church Wardens were appointed as Pest Controllers and a bounty of 3d. per bundle of rats' tails was paid to enterprising parishioners who had been known to include a few mouse tails in their bundles, so, to counter this ungodly conduct, a minimum of 1½ inches was stipulated. In seed sowing time, sparrows' masks were added to the church warden's list of criminals 'wanted'. Careful church records were kept of the money paid out for these services – when the tithe system was discarded and the churches compensated by grants of lands from which rents could produce comparable incomes, these duties of Church-wardens passed into secular hands and Rat and Sparrow Clubs were started – quite social affairs, whose members met for 'Count nights' in the 'local'. In 1960 a few such clubs still existed in Kent.

The problem of a clean water supply to cities began to be taken seriously in the mid-century and as drinking water improved the incidence of Cholera and Typhus diminished. It is noticeable also that tea drinking contributed vastly to the nation's better health, as the water for brewing it had to be boiled. But for the very poor, the price of tea was prohibitive until late Victorian days when Indian grown teas came into the market.

Chapter 5

A Visit to Sheffield

JULY 1st. Today a servant of cousin Benjamin arrived with a letter for Mother,[1] asking if I might visit them. The maid is to be in Wakefield for a few days and Mrs. Benjamin suggests that if I might go to Sheffield on the day of her return she could attend me. To my delight and surprise Mother agreed to the arrangement.

July 3rd. Mother and I went into town and I bought 12 yards of silk for a frock and we called at Miss Williamson's to tell her to come to sew next week. The town is very busy preparing for the elections for the new Reform Parliament. Two candidates have offered themselves for Wakefield; Mr. Daniel Gaskell of Lupset Hall and C. Gascoigne of Pollington Hall. Mr. Gaskell is to address a Public Meeting this evening.

July 9th. Cousin Benjamin's maid Eliza called for me and we took the eleven o'clock stage-coach. We changed horses at Barnsley and arrived in Sheffield at half-past-two. In the coach I sat opposite a young lady accompanied by an elderly person. I looked at her for a long time wondering where and when I had seen her before, then I suddenly realized that it was myself she resembled. It was quite strange. At Sheffield we were met by cousin Benjamin. Their house is called 'Broomfield Cottage' and it has a charming garden surrounded by fields and farm lands. Mrs. T. C. arrived soon after I did, she seems to have invited herself and I fancy Mrs. Benjamin is not too pleased about it.

July 10th. I wrote to Mother. It was raining all morning and I read 'Ivanhoe'. Benjamin's cousins Richard and

Ellen Bayley called and I gave Richard my letter to send to Wakefield. He is a very stout, good looking young man of about thirty and seems very good tempered. His sister is quite different. She is tall and thin and fair haired and looks not very good tempered.

July 11th. Went with Mrs. Benjamin and Mrs. T. C. into town to do some shopping and then to call on Mr. and Mrs. Bayley (Mr. Bayley is the brother of my aunt Thomas). Richard and Ellen then went with us to the Music Hall where there was an anti-slavery meeting. Mr. Montgomery, the poet, was in the chair. All the clergy and ministers in the town were there and the four candidates for the coming elections in Sheffield. They were Messrs. Buckingham, Samuel Bayley, Ward and Parker. There was a Mr. Thompson from the Parent Society in London whom I liked very well. They all spoke and it was a very long meeting. Mrs. T. C. became ill and nearly fainted and Richard had to help her. He took her home and by the time we arrived she seemed quite well again. Mrs. Benjamin thinks it was just affectation. However, she went to bed early and Mrs. Benjamin and I walked in the garden. Henry Clarkson called on his way from the Rotherham sessions. He was in one of his most haughty moods, so I was just as haughty.

July 12th. Reading 'Ivanhoe' in the morning. We dined at the Bayley's in Norfolk Street. Mr. and Mrs. Walker were there. Mr. Walker is Mrs. Benjamin's Uncle. They invited us all to spend a few days with them at Crook Hill Hall and Mr. Bayley said he would drive us there. After dinner we played the piano for a while and when we arrived home we found my mother there. My letter had not arrived and she had been so uneasy about me that she had determined to come to Sheffield to see if all was well.

July 13th. Went into town with Mother, Mrs. Benjamin and Mrs. T. C. The shops are much cheaper here than in Wakefield. We saw some lovely specimens of Sheffield cutlery and scissors and Mother bought a pen knife for Alfred.[2]

July 14th. Mother returned by coach to Wakefield and she says I may remain here until Monday two weeks. Mr. Bayley came and drove us to Crook Hill Hall. It is 13 miles from Sheffield, about half way between Rotherham and Doncaster. I never saw a more beautiful countryside. The Hall is situated in a lovely park and the grounds are excellently laid out. The house itself is handsome and the rooms are enormous and elegantly furnished. Mary Walker, a niece, is visiting there from York. She is about nineteen, a very pretty girl and genteel looking. Mrs. T. C. became ill and had to retire to bed quite early. Richard, Mary, Frederick and Robert and I played Giraffe in the garden until quite late.

July 15th. Sunday. Mrs. T. C. seemed quite well again. Mary and I walked in the garden early and gathered rosebuds to wear in our hair. We were soon joined by Richard who began to pay great attention to Mary. We walked up and down the drive which is a beautiful avenue with great trees and over half a mile long. After breakfast we strolled in the gardens and did not go to church. After dinner we played the piano and sang duets and later we walked to Ellingham Woods and I was quite shocked to see Richard walk with his arm around Mary's waist and when we were in the woods I saw him kiss her, yet they met only a few days ago. Ellingham Woods are very extensive and there are clearings and pathways. It was a rather overcast and gloomy evening and we sat in an arbour and were served with Porter and old Mr. Bayley smoked a pipe. Mary is one of those people who stop at nothing and to prove it she took a pipe and filled it with tobacco and smoked it. I felt very sorry indeed to see her do so and I think that even Richard was shocked. It was very late when we got home and I had felt most uncomfortable all day to think that we should spend Sunday as we had done and I wondered what Mother would have said.

July 15th. In the garden early with Mary and found Richard waiting there. The boys had a swing fixed between two high trees and they said that every time they swang as high as a certain very high branch Mary must kiss them and she agreed, and of course she had many kisses. I thought it a most indelicate thing to permit. Robert tried to persuade me to let them swing me but I would not let them. They laughed famously at my refusal but I did not care and when I told Mrs. Benjamin and Mrs. T. C. later they said how prudent they thought me, for young ladies should not swing in the presence of gentlemen. After breakfast we set off in two gigs for Roche Abbey. It is about 7 miles from Crook Hill Hall and is on an estate belonging to the Earl of Scarbro'. The abbey is in the midst of an immense wood. It is in ruins and very little of it remains. There is a river quite close and the woods are beautifully kept. We walked many miles and drove back for dinner at four o'clock.

July 17th. In the garden, swinging and kissing again just like yesterday. After breakfast we all went for a picnic in a hay field. Richard and Mary left us and were away together for quite an hour. After dinner we drove to Doncaster; I admired the town. We saw the racecourse and then we drove to Conisbro'[3] which is only about one mile from Crook Hill. Mrs. Walker's sister lives there and it is the prettiest and most romantic looking village I ever saw. The house in which Mr. and Mrs. P. live is quite close to the ruins of Conisbro Castle which is interesting to me because Sir Walter Scott makes it the setting of much of his novel of Ivanhoe. The castle was built before the Norman Conquest and there is very little of it left now, except the keep, which is completely round and three stories high. We climbed a long flight of steps to the second storey and walked on a projection only about a yard wide, the others walked all round but not I. They went up to the third storey and walked again on that projecting ledge but I was afraid. It looked most dangerous and it was late day and growing dark too. We arrived home for late dinner and Mrs. T. C. retired to her room, not feeling well. The rest of us danced quadrilles, folk dances and reels. Frederick was my partner most of the time and we had a most agreeable time. Mrs. Benjamin told me that Mrs. T. C. is not ill but that her real trouble is gin. I had heard some rumour of this before but of course had seen nothing of it – it is very shocking if it is true.

July 20th. Returned to Broomfield Cottage.

July 22nd. Sunday. Spent the day with Mr. and Mrs. Bayley. I went with Ellen to church in the morning and again in the afternoon. It was the old parish church and the Vicar preached. As we walked home in the afternoon I told Ellen that I was a Unitarian and she seemed quite shocked. I suppose I should have mentioned it sooner but I really thought she knew. I felt a little hurt by her manner.

July 23rd. We visited a friend of the Bayleys who is about the same age as my mother yet she goes without a cap in the house. She has a tall and tolerably handsome son and they tell me she is afraid of inviting young ladies to the house as she says 'Poor Robert is so susceptible to love!'.

July 24th. Busy today making hyacinths from coloured paper to put in the fire places for Mrs. Benjamin. Then Ellen came and we took a long walk to Crook's Moor. The country around Sheffield really is very beautiful. Mary Walker is coming to stay at Norfolk Street next week and they want me to stay too but I dare not. Mother said to return next Monday.

July 25th. Making hyacinths and I showed Ellen how to make them. Later we went to Norfolk Street. Ellen's two elder sisters had just arrived home from Liverpool. Elizabeth is very like Richard and quite good looking. On the way home we bought more coloured paper for hyacinths.

July 27th. Mrs. Benjamin was very ill again today so lay on the sofa and read. I took a long walk with cousin Benjamin to a place called Hincliffe.

July 29th. Sunday. I had a bad cold and did not feel well but cousin Benjamin and I went to St. Georges Church and sat with the Stentons who are great friends of the

Bayleys. The Vicar preached a sermon about the Cholera. In the afternoon Mary and Mrs. Benjamin and I went for a long walk to a small village called Norton and there we had tea at a small inn where there was the prettiest serving maid.

July 30th. Packed my things and prepared to return home. They wanted me very much to stay longer but I did not dare, but I was sorry to go and wept famously as we parted. Just as the coach was leaving I saw a man in the Cholera. They were wheeling him on a cart to the hospital. His limbs seemed quite contorted and he looked a most miserable object. His arms were drawn upwards and he was the picture of death. In the coach the people talked of little else but the Cholera and I was quite frightened. Eliza accompanied me and is to stay a few days in Wakefield. Mother and Alfred were glad of my return but Mother says she would have been angry had I been persuaded to stay longer.

[1] Mention is frequently made in the journal, of letters being carried by servants or 'per kind favour' of a friend. There was a national postal service at that time but it had many disadvantages. It was slow and often unreliable. One sheet of paper only might be used and writing restricted to one side of that sheet. Envelopes had not yet come into use and the sheet was folded with writing inside and the address written on the reverse and secured with a wafer or wax seal. The wafer was considered just a little 'non U'. It also had the disadvantage of being easily removed and re-affixed which could not happen with a wax seal. Once broken that could not be restored to its original condition and was therefore a better guarantee of privacy. The recipient of the letter paid the charges, about nine-pence per letter for short distances, 1/6 for longer journeys and if anything were enclosed, the charge was doubled. Envelopes came into use in 1840 at the same time as postage stamps and the sender affixed the stamp which cost one penny only. Stamps were called 'Queen's heads' and they were not on perforated sheets, but had to be cut out with scissors. This penny post continued in England for about 100 years.

[2] Pen knives were so called because they were used to cut or repair quill pens.

[3] Conisbro Castle was one of five Roman strongpoints on the road between London and Edinbro'. It was restored and strengthened by the Normans.

Chapter 6

Slavery

THE entry about the anti-slavery meeting in Sheffield on July 11th is the one and only reference to the slave question which I have found in the journals. There may have been mention of it in the missing volumes but from the tone of the report on the July meeting, one gets the impression that Clara's interest in slavery was very superficial, and that is rather astonishing, as Thomas Clarkson was her father's cousin and also because Yorkshire was the stronghold of the movement from its earliest stages.

The English trade in slaves dates back to the reign of Elizabeth I and was a development from the ivory trade which had been going on since about 1528 with the friendly negroes of the Guinea Coast. In Elizabeth's reign it occurred to the traders that 'black cargo' might be just as profitable as ivory. Trade then took a new turn. Instead of bartering trinkets with the coast dwellers for ivory, the traders went inland, and there native tribal chiefs sold men, women and children for guns, hardware, cotton cloth and spirits. But it was not a really big business until the continental wars when France, Spain and Portugal lost much of their sea power to Britain. By 1770 it was estimated that some 50,000 slaves were transported annually by British ships from Africa to the Americas and to Jamaica and Haiti.

The purchased slaves were manacled and marched to the sea coast, the sick or injured being abandoned by the wayside to fall prey to wild beasts or die of hunger and thirst. It was said that the paths to the coast were littered with human bones. At the coast they were sorted out and again the weak or damaged were abandoned and the rest packed into the waiting transports in conditions indescribably horrible, so filthy, cramped and airless that about half the 'cargo' died on the 'middle passage' and were thrown overboard. Arriving in port the survivors were patched up and auctions were held. Any weak, very young or unattractive types being sold cheap at the end, in composite lots, as 'refuse'. On the plantations, life was so miserable that not many survived for more than a few years. They were badly fed, badly housed, overworked and beaten and often tortured. There has been no equal to this mass murder and human degradation except perhaps in the death camps of Hitler, such as Auschwitz and Buchenwald.

In the year 1772 there were about 15,000 slaves actually owned in England and slave sales were held in English ports, chiefly London, Liverpool and Bristol. The iron rings to which slaves were chained are still to be seen embedded in the walls along the dockside in Liverpool. England seems to have always harboured a fundamental dislike of slavery and slave trading. The first real step towards its abolition occurred in 1767 when Grenville Sharp had a law-suit against a slave owner in regard to a slave named 'Somerset'. After lengthy hearings the legal decision of Lord Mansfield was that once a slave set foot on English soil he became a free man. But a law-court decision is not a 'law' and Granville Sharp and others called on the government to have Lord Mansfield's ruling placed in the Statute Book.

The sugar plantations of Jamaica were almost entirely British owned and depended on slave labour, and British Merchant shipping had a near monopoly on the slave transport trade between the African coast and America. The Navy depended chiefly on 'press gang' sailors and on its many slaves. Parliament was therefore most reluctant to sabotage its navy or merchant fleet and its rich investments in sugar to a little scruple about the rights and wrongs of slave trading.

It took courage to start an anti-slavery movement two hundred years ago, just when the trade was at its peak of profit, but Granville Sharp and his fellow reformers were brave men. Theirs was a courage born of righteousness, intellectual integrity and pity. Amongst these were such great men as John Wesley, Adam Smith, Dr. Johnson, Zachaias

Macauly, James Ramsey and many others of like calibre, most of them Quakers, Methodists or Evangelicals. Cambridge University was their springboard. In 1785 Thomas Clarkson won the University prize for a Latin essay on the theme 'Is it right to make men slaves against their will?'. This essay, translated into English, attracted much attention to the question of slavery and stimulated activity in that reform movement. William Wilberforce, who had been interested in Evangelicals and anti-slavery during his Cambridge days had been one of the two M.P.'s for Yorkshire since 1784 and now he joined the crusade whole-heartedly. When, in 1797, a committee was formed to prepare a Bill for Parliament, Granville Sharp was its President and William Wilberforce and Thomas Clarkson were his vice-Presidents. From then on Wilberforce devoted all his energy and his great charm and eloquence to press the cause in Parliament. Pitt was then Prime Minister and because of his life-long friendship with Wilberforce, did nothing to hinder the movement, though he could not be said to have fostered it greatly. The home of Wilberforce in Clapham became the centre for the anti-slavery campaign and he and his coterie were often referred to as 'the saints' – not without a slight hint of derision. Thomas Clarkson was the one who directed the propaganda side of the crusade and he collected much of the irrefutable evidence. He journeyed on a 'slaver' in the notorious 'middle passage' to find out transport conditions for himself and journeyed twice to Paris during the Terror in an effort to gain French support. There was a misplaced hope in those days that the French Revolution was to be a bid for human freedom and happiness everywhere, no matter what colour the skin might be. It was a bitter disappointment to find that it developed into a bestial hate of aristocrats by peasants and underdogs. England had never experienced that bitter antagonism between the land-owner and the land-worker. Some people believe that had the French aristocrats played cricket on the village greens with tenants and villagers as the young nobility and gentry of England did, there would have been fewer heads roll before the guillotine.

The organisation of publicity and propaganda for causes such as Parliamentary reform and anti-slavery was quite astonishing in an age without railways, telephones or even a 'penny post'. It was achieved by pamphleteering, lecture tours and sermons – the latter almost exclusively in non-conformist churches.

Pitt died in 1806 and Fox became Prime Minister. The first anti-slavery Act was passed in the following year. It was a great achievement but it was not enough, as it applied only to the slave trade in Britain.

The next step was to increase the scope of the Bill to cover British overseas territories. In 1818 Thomas Clarkson presented a petition to Alexander I of Russia who promised support of the cause of liberation of existing slaves in territories other than British. When Wilberforce retired from Parliament in 1825 (due to failing health) he persuaded a Mr. T. Fowell Buxton to take his place as pleader of the cause in the House. Fowell Buxton had become M.P. in 1818. He was a young man and in many ways quite the opposite of Wilberforce, who was small, fragile and gentle in manner; Buxton was huge, healthy and forceful in style, but no better choice could have been made. He came of Quaker stock and had all the zeal and enthusiasm of the pioneers in the movement. More and more writers, poets and men of influence became supporters of the cause and a young man named Whitely (a Yorkshire man) wrote of things he had seen whilst on a visit to Jamaica and his story roused public feeling to a new heat. Newspapers, which had hitherto been silent, joined in the outcry.

The second Abolition of Slavery Act was one of the first bills passed by the new Reformed Parliament on August 29th 1833 and the Act came into effect from the 31st July 1834. The sum of twenty million pounds was paid to the sugar planters of Jamaica by way of compensation – a staggering amount of money in those days. Wilberforce died just one month before the passing of the Bill but he followed all the Parliamentary discussions and one of his last remarks was 'Thank God that I should have lived to witness the day on

Conisbro' or Coningsborough Castle and small chapel in foreground, from a drawing made in 1770. The ancient name was Caer Canon, later changed to Coning Byrgh.

which England is willing to pay twenty million sterling for the abolition of slavery'. The effect of the 1833 Act was no magic transformation which ended abuse there and then. A demand for slaves still existed in non-British countries, chiefly in the cotton states of America, Mexico and Peru. There were plenty of pirate ships ready to take risks, for the reduced supply sent up the prices. Difficulty of replacement often meant that one slave was forced to do the work of two. At the risk of being accused of punning, it could truly be said that a 'black market' in slaves came into existence which was highly lucrative and flourished for a very long time. In the year 1870 'Black Birding' was in full swing in the Pacific and was still going on in the first quarter of the present century. It is true that latterly they did not buy or sell the 'blackbirds', they only borrowed them, sometimes by force, and repatriated them after a limited period, giving them small sums of money for accumulated wages. This money no doubt served as conscience salve for the employer but was of little or no value to the forced labourer when back in his primitive home land.

Of all those who crusaded in the anti-slavery campaign, perhaps the most dynamic was Granville Sharp, yet his name is seldom mentioned nowadays. He was born in 1735 of a good Yorkshire family and was a man of great learning. Not only was he the founder of the Anti-Slavery Society in 1791 but he also founded the British and Foreign Bible Society and a Society for Conversion of the Jews. He was one of the most prominent people in the founding of the state of Sierra Leone as a national home for liberated or runaway slaves. He fought for Parliamentary reform, Irish Independence and against the horrid operations of the 'press gangs'. Few men have done more for their fellows than he did. He died, aged 78, in 1813. There is some irony in the fact that the slave trade was carried on in Sierra Leone until it was finally outlawed in 1926.

It is an odd thing that nowadays one frequently hears Wilberforce referred to as 'Bishop Wilberforce'. Even the late André Maurois in his very good 'History of England' makes this mistake. Bishop Wilberforce was Samuel, son of

William. William Wilberforce was an Evangelical and a layman. His burial in Westminster Abbey may have been a gesture by the Establishment to a cause which it had done little to help when help was most needed and no doubt gave more satisfaction to Samuel the Bishop than it would have given to William the Emancipator. Had William Wilberforce been an average man he might have become Prime Minister of England after his great friend Pitt's death in 1806, for he had the charm and the ability and came from the social order from which Prime Ministers were drawn in those days, but he had no self-interest or personal ambitions. Thomas Clarkson died at the age of 76 in the year 1846. He was buried in the church yard quite close to his lovely old home, a moated manor house at Playford near Ipswich in East Anglia.

Fowell Buxton, later knighted, was also a Quaker of good family. He married Hannah Gurney, sister of Elizabeth Fry, well remembered on account of her work for Prison Reform. Buxton was associated with every good cause in an age of great causes and of great reforms. It was he, who in 1822 piloted Richard Martin's Animal Protection Act through Parliament.

The emancipation of slaves was not the work of any one man. It was a magnificent example of team work and of the might of organised public opinion.

The place of slaves in naval and merchant ships was taken by so-called 'paid' labourers, Lascars (Indian sailors) often 'liberated' slaves and this type of crew was employed until very recent times. They were badly fed, badly housed, badly treated and were the last to leave the ship in distress, often being held below deck at gun point.

Nasty as the general principle of slavery may be, it has a credit side which should not be lost sight of in entirety. The human animal is no labour lover; he is by nature slow-moving, indolent and passive. The dynamic types are rare. Slavery imposed work on the unwilling – it made possible the progress planned by master minds which would otherwise have been left undone. Eventually it may have altered the mental attitude of the common man towards labour. The idea of 'the dignity of labour' had to be bred into the mind of civilised man and no doubt slavery helped. It also helped to eliminate the evil practice of cannibalism, for the eating of one's enemy did not get one very far; a meal or two and the situation was back to its grim subsistence level. But a slave was good for many a day's work and that meant better living. It altered the whole picture. It was the foundation stone of civilisation and culture; so out of evil came good to the whole of mankind. The sad part of the story is that having climbed out of the depth and breathed the clean air and seen the sun and the stars, man does not know how to use his glorious and hardwon heritage. He has grasped the idea of liberty and has a glimmer about equality but the meaning of fraternity still eludes him. Is it so much better to burn your neighbour with napalm and kill him with strontium 90 than to slay him with a club?

Sometime, somewhere in this world, there should be a magnificent monument erected to slavery and to all those slaves who lived and died to make possible the imperfect degree of civilisation which we now enjoy. And someday the question may well be asked, 'Was the product worth the price?'. If 'Black Power' ever wipes every white man from the face of the earth, it will inherit the gains and it cannot escape some of the blame, for slavery existed amongst the black races themselves long before the Western world took over the vile traffic. One fact should never be overlooked: at a time when the slave trade was at its most profitable, it was Englishmen who denounced it. They fought an evil thing and theirs is the everlasting honour, for as Lecky, the historian wrote, 'The unweary, unostentatious, inglorious crusade of England against slavery may probably be regarded as amongst the three or four perfectly virtuous pages comprised in the history of nations'.

Chapter 7

The Wakefield Soke

AUGUST 6th. There is great excitement in town celebrating the passing of the Reform Bill, and there is to be a dinner in Wakefield for 1,200 people today. We all went to Mr. Barff's and sat with them in their summer house to watch the processions as they passed along Westgate. There were bands playing everywhere and great rejoicings.

August 8th. Henriette and Mary Staniland called and I lent them my book on fortunetelling. Then we went to call on Mrs. Burton, they are very uncomfortable again, for William is drinking and behaving very ill and causing disturbances. Mrs. B. and dear Eb wept about it.

August 13th. Eb called to say goodbye as she is going on a visit to Hull and will be away for about three weeks. I wept at our parting.

August 16th. Mr. Scatcherd sent his carriage for us. It had rained since early morning but it cleared later and I was able to play in the garden with Fanny and Watson and to walk in the orchard. Then Mrs. S. and Mother and I called on Mrs. John Webster. Mr. and Mrs. Brook came whilst we were there and they were talking of Mr. Walker's workpeople who have all thrown out.[1]

August 19th. Sunday. We went to church and Mr. Cassel preached an excellent sermon. He and the Scatcherds are not friendly just now. After church I walked with Adelle and Virginia Wills, they are very frenchified and quite amusing. After dinner Mr. S. read us a poem, 'The meridian of Morley' in which he makes fun of all their neighbours, and I do believe the nasty creature wrote it in church this morning.

August 20th. Mrs. S., Mother and Watson and I walked to Wood Church and called on Mr. Hepworth, who is the clergyman there. His wife is a kinswoman of Mrs. S. He is a very handsome man of about sixty. He is a very good listener, but he never says anything but 'yes' or 'no' or 'how very true' or 'yes indeed'. The church is in ruins. They showed us the stalls of the Black Cannons and everyone admired it very much, in fact, they spent nearly two hours doing so, but I saw little to admire and I had a headache. I was very tired when we got back home for it was a long walk.

August 21st. There was an evening party at the Staniland's. Everyone sang solos or duets or played the piano. Adelle has such a strong voice and she never knows when she has exerted it sufficiently and she quavers on every note as if she were being shaken. I declare, I was quite electrified. After some loud piano playing we all settled down to Backgammon.

August 26th. Very busy copying music of 'Now at Moonlights Fair Hour'. I had to make haste as I wished to finish it before we set off for home. Mrs. S. came to Wakefield with us, and James (the groom) drove us as Mr. S. was not very well. After dining with Alfred we went to town and called to enquire about Eb who came back from Hull so ill that she had to be bled. However, she is much better and she gave me some heads cut out of paper to show on the wall by candlelight. I showed her how to make a chain of silk braid, as I was shown at Morley a few days ago.

August 27th. I went with Jane and Mary to Flanshaw, and we saw the Alverthorpe Sunday scholars walk.[2] Jane told me as a very great secret that her Uncle Samuel is going to marry a young Greek lady and he has written to his father (old Mr. Barff) to ask his consent. They are all most provoked as they had expected he would leave his fortune to them.

August 29th. I saw them take someone to the Cholera hospital today. It begins to be very bad in Wakefield now.

Nine new cases on Westgate Common and Mr. Shepherd, Governor of the prison, is dead of it.

September 3rd. Mother and I went to town and chose our new bonnets at Miss Duckworth's. Mine is a very pretty shape, rather open and it turns up a little at the back. We saw a procession of the 'Odd Fellows' and when we got home we found Mr. and Mrs. Webster and Elizabeth Asquith there. They had wine and cake before going back to Morley.

September 6th. My Aunt and Uncle Wood came and Captain and Mrs. Dawson, Henry and John. There was great talk of all the news in town and Henry (as usual) said nasty things about Jocinians, and my Aunt Wood was no better. They both said that our congregation was so small because of Mr. Johnstone's old sermons and so I assured them that we all liked them and admired Mr. Johnstone greatly.

September 8th. Alfred was very ill today. We sent for Mr. Ebineza Walker and he gave him something which seemed to do him good, but we were very much afraid that it might be the Cholera.

September 9th. Sunday. Alfred is much better but had a bad night and must remain in bed. William Johnstone came to visit him and played several pieces of sacred music. Eb went to chapel with me, and seems quite well again. I had the toothache and tried oil of cloves but it did no good at all.

September 10th. Went to a large party at my Uncle Wood's, and all the conversation was about the Doncaster recess. Later we played various games but I had the toothache and was glad to come home. Dear Mother gave me some brandy to hold to my tooth and it quite cured it.

September 14th. My Uncle John and Henry are away in York. My uncle is having a court trial with Haigh and Lindsey, something about the Soke.[3] It is likely to be a very expensive affair even if my uncle wins and the family are very concerned about it and keeping indoors, and not allowing the doors to be answered or opened as they fear a subpoena from the Haigh side, asking Mary or Lawrance to go to York to testify about a signature which they do not wish to do.

[1] The term 'throw out' was used to describe what we now call 'a strike'.

[2] The Sunday School 'walks' are mentioned in Jane Austen's novels and seem to have been a type of religious advertising. The only schools available for the children of the poor were, in those days, either Sunday schools or Charity schools. Sunday schools were first started by the non-conformist churches but later the Church of England adopted the system. In these schools the children were taught to read and even to write by public spirited young men and women of the congregation and such instruction was the only education most of them ever received. Charity schools were, as a rule, endowed by landowners for the benefit of their tenants and were generally in rural areas. The Clarkson Charity School was one of this type, founded in Mansfield in 1725. The conditions were that boys and girls be taught to read, but boys only, be taught to write. However, the girls were taught to sew and spin and every girl was provided with a spinning wheel which became her very own property. At that time, to own a spinning wheel was more profitable than the ability to write, for few, if any, of them would ever be required to write so much as her own name.

[3] There is no further mention of this affair in the journal, but Henry Clarkson's Memoires throw light on the subject of 'Soke'. The word does not occur in modern dictionaries but the *Encyclopaedia Britannica* gives about two inches of explanation. It says that the word came into use in England following the Norman Conquest and a very precise definition of its meaning is difficult to pinpoint. It could imply the right to hold court and give judgement or it could mean jurisdiction over an area of land or over an industry or trade with rights to impose and collect fees and fines. It is a system of French origin and no doubt the tradition of 'droit de Seignieur' which existed in France, started as a type of 'soke'. The monopoly in glass-making was another example of the soke system. In that country, only people who were granted Royal Privilege had the right to own glass factories. They were known as 'gentilhommes verriers' – the system came to England and was a monopoly often granted to Court favourites, clergy or powerful nobles, the Duke of Buckingham being one of the latter variety. The right of the Dukes of Leeds to exact poll tax at the Wakefield cattle market was a 'soke'.

The soke to which Clara referred on September 14th concerned a flour milling tax. Henry Clarkson writes in his memoirs, 'This was the Wakefield Soke and I have been favoured with the sight of a legal document which gives the particulars of this ancient privilege, granted by James I to a certain Robert Hungate and Henry Foxcroft and their heirs forever, in return for which they paid the sum of fifty-pounds to the Duchy of Lancaster. There were three soke mills altogether, the principal one at Wakefield, and two smaller ones at Horbury and Newmiller dam – or the New-Mill-at-the-Dam, as it is called in the Act. The soke obliged the inhabitants of certain townships – Wakefield, Alverthorpe, Thornes, Horbury, Ossett, Stanley, Crigglestone and Sandal to grind all their corn at one of the soke mills and moreover prohibited them from using any flour that had been ground elsewhere. The only persons exempt from this vexatious obligation were those holding property which had formerly been in possession of the Knights Templars or Knights of St. John, who might grind their corn when and where they liked. The Wakefield soke passed into the hands of the Pilkington family who let it on lease till the final purchase by the town in 1853 for the sum of eighteen thousand pounds which was paid by a rate extending over six years. The township of Ossett had thrown off the yoke in about

1830 and purchased its exemption for the sum of three thousand five hundred pounds. The Grant states that the fishery in the river near the mill was expressly reserved for the owners of the soke, a privilege not to be lightly esteemed in the days when the Calder was a fine salmon stream.' This restriction on fishing, together with the existing game laws, pressed heavily on the hungry, underprivileged working folk and penalties for poaching fish or game were disproportionately severe. The word 'soc' or 'soke' has passed out of the English language and is found only in a few place names such as Thorpe-le-soken, Soke of Peterborough and Eton Soke. We have still, however, a colloquial expression which derives from the system – 'to be soked or soaked', meaning to be cheated or overcharged.

Chapter 8

Local Affairs and Lead Coffins

SEPTEMBER 23rd. Sunday. A Mr. Marriott preached twice. In the morning, on 'the duty of self examination' and the second was a continuation of the first, in answer to the assertion 'that man is inherently wicked'. I liked it very much but Eb did not and I think did not thank me for having taken her to our Chapel.

September 24th. Mother and cousin Ann and Mrs. W. and I went to a lecture at the Court House by Mr. Marriott on Social Economy. Mr. Marriott is the gentleman who preached yesterday and his parish is near Warrington. He has a wife and four children and has only sixty-five pounds a year and the poor man is obliged to do something to keep them.[1] We paid two shillings each and he talked of food, clothing and education. He descends to the every-day affairs of life and his lecture was written in rather a homely style but contained a good deal of sound sense. It lasted for two hours and Alfred called for us to take us home afterwards.

October 19th. Mr. and Mrs. Scatcherd, Watson and Fanny came and dined with us then we went to a house in Wood St. where Mrs. Scatcherd got her profile[2] in black taken. Watson had one taken too. Then we called at the library and got 'Waverly' for Mrs. Scatcherd and I got 'The Last of the Mohicans'. When we came home we found Mrs. Benjamin there. She is visiting at Newmillerdam. One of Cousin Thomas's pupils had driven her over. She says she has been feeling ill for some weeks and would have liked to have had me to stay with her but as the Cholera was so bad in Sheffield they thought that Mother might not allow me to go.

October 23rd. The tenant at Hardwick paid the rent today of which Mother was very glad. Mary Jane and Eb and Mother and I played several pools of quadrille and William came to take Eb home at half past seven, then he was going to Sandal to bring home his father, who is having one of his drinking fits there.

October 28th. Mr. Johnstone preached on 'Isaac meditating in the fields', with variations and additions, one of his very oldest sermons.

October 29th. Miss Williamson is here to sew for a few days. She is making new morning frocks for Mother and for me and altering some of dear Father's shirts to fit Alfred.

October 30th. Mother and I went to a lecture at the Court House by Dr. Alexander on the character of Napoleon Bonapart and on the evils of war. It was given for the benefit of the Mechanic's Institute. It was very long and very dry.

November 12th. Wakefield Fair. Went with Mary Ann and Jane to old Mr. Barff's and at 9 o'clock my Uncle John came for me. When we got to our gate he said to go on by myself, and he would stand and hold up the lantern until I went indoors. But I had not gone many yards when I could not see the lantern at all and it was with the greatest difficulty that I found the door and I was very much frightened.

November 13th. It was so dark all day today. We had to burn candles all the time. Hannah's brother came to tell her that he had married recently.

November 19th. My Aunt Wood called. She told us that Mr. Gilby (the surgeon) is leaving Wakefield for Bristol; we are all very sorry but he has been very unpopular here since the sad affair of the little chimney boy. People blamed him for delay in ordering the chimney to be dismantled and when at last they did so the poor little boy was dead from asphyxiation.

November 20th. Today is dear Eb's birthday; she is twenty-four. Henry is drinking a good deal and last night caused quite a disturbance. William did the same thing a few nights ago. Eb and her mother wept bitterly about it. The men of their family are a sad disappointment to them.

November 25th. Went to town with Mother but we met cousin Ann in Westgate so I went with her, and Mother went to arrange about her new bonnet. Ann was as oddly dressed as usual – a morning frock and red shawl and black muff; she was looking for a new gardener. She told me that my Aunt Wood is quite ill and they know it is because she ate some pork which they all advised her not to eat, but she did, and so deserves little pity.

December 1st. My aunt Wood is very ill indeed but at first they thought she must have died.

December 3rd. We are having our bonnets altered; they are being worn quite small – just the reverse of the former style. I cannot reconcile myself to such smallness. Called at my Uncle John's with the newspaper.

December 12th. Mr. Daniel Gaskell was today declared elected as the first M.P. for Wakefield. He was chaired at the Court House and carried around the town in a chair made especially for the occasion, upholstered in orange velvet – the Whig colour. My Aunt Wood is still very weak and has to be carried up or down stairs.

December 20th. Today is the final day of the elections for two members for the West Riding. It is the first time that voting for the Riding has taken place in Wakefield.[3] Mother and I went to the Court House in spite of having bad colds. My cough was very bad but I could not consent to stay home. There were hustings erected, but we stood with several other ladies in the Court Yard, a little aside. We heard most of Lord Morpeth's speech and Mr. Staniland's. Several other gentlemen spoke and a person called Godfrey Higgins was a kind of opposition. Mr. Staniland and Lord Morpeth were declared elected and then we came home and did not wait for the chairing, for it was perishingly cold. There was a great Public Breakfast and a procession in honour of the High Sheriff.

December 23rd. Sunday. Mother and I had very bad colds so did not go to Chapel. I read two sermons.

December 25th. Christmas Day. Reading and doing embroidery and stayed indoors all day.

December 26th. Uncle John and aunt Wood and seven cousins came to dine. I half begin to imagine that Alfred likes Mary Ann just a little – just the least little bit in the world. She teases him and scolds him and he seems to enjoy it. Jane is the one who is always in love with some-one – at present it is with her mother's physician. He is more than twice her age, very tall and very stout; so stout that he has several times broken his gig with his great weight. He is moreover a widower with two children, but Jane is deeply in love and imagines he loves her. Of course Jane is determined to be married before her sisters or cousins. We played card games and then danced quadrilles and were most agreeable.

December 27th. Called on my aunt Thomas. Some time ago, because of fear of thieves, she had hidden a large bank note in an armchair and then she could not find it again, so today she got a carpenter to take the chair to pieces and he found it for her. She told us that when she dies she has directed in her will that she be put in a lead coffin and left for two weeks[4] in the crypt of the church, until she be spoiled, and then she is to be buried in the family vault.

[1] The stipends of clergy were at that time most urgently in need of adjustment. Some clergy had parishes with miserably small incomes, others had large incomes and little or no parishes. The Rev. Peter Jackson of Castlelodge, near Wake-field, had no parish at all and lived the life of a sporting squire. Such anomalies were commonplace. Some clergy even held several endowments whilst others lived on the bread-line. Livings were generally in the gift of the landowner and the better endowed ones frequently reserved for younger sons or sons-in-law. Such clergymen were sometimes spoken of as 'squarsons'. In the year 1838 there were 4,000 non-resident Church of England parsons in England.

[2] Black Profiles, usually called 'silhouettes', were so named after Etienne de Silhouette, Controller General of France in 1767. It was by way of an economy that he had these profiles made of his family; they cost so much less than full portraits, and it was in derision that outline likenesses were given his name and by his name such outlines are still described.

[3] Until this time, Yorkshire, the largest county in England, sent only 2 mem-bers to Westminster. There was only one polling booth for the whole county and that was in the Castle Yard at York. The election campaign usually lasted about three weeks and during that time electors were conveyed to the polling booth at the expense of the candidate by post-chaise, carriage, or canal barge

Black profile of 'dearest mother' taken in Wood Street in 1832.

and all hospitality of board and refreshment were free to the voter. It is reputed to have cost every candidate at least one-hundred-thousand pounds to contest an election. Only landowners had a vote and the bigger landowners had several votes each, dependent on the location of their various properties.

In the reformed Parliament, representation was based on density of population, most of the 'rotten' and 'pocket' boroughs were eliminated. The franchise was extended to include leaseholder, copy-holders and householders of town property valued at more than 10 pounds a year. This liberalisation was jubilantly welcomed throughout the land, yet it still left 21 people out of every 22 without a vote. It brought about no sudden change in the type or style of members of Parliament, but from this date the members knew that they represented not just places, but people.

[4] The instruction about the two weeks in the crypt or 'until she be spoiled' was simply a precaution against being buried alive – a very unpleasant experience which happened more frequently in the past than it does today. The expression 'to turn in his grave' was at one time not just a figure of speech. Many unfortunate creatures did so. It was said that when the Church of Rome considered a canonisation, it was usual, if at all possible, to exhume and view the corpse. If there were any signs of post burial disturbance, indicating an awakening and frenzied attempts to escape, the candidate was disqualified on the grounds of unsaintly display of temper. Until quite recent days many people directed in their wills that a vein in the wrist be severed before burial as a precaution against such an awakening. It was not until 1842 that compulsory notification of births or deaths was introduced and no medical certificates of death were required before a funeral until the year 1848.

The direction about the lead coffin needed much more consideration. The wooden coffin which we take for granted today did not come into use in England until the late 17th century, and lead, zinc or stone continued to be favoured until a very much later date. The word 'coffin' comes from the Greek word 'Kophinos' meaning 'a crust' or 'a basket' or 'a covering'. Prehistoric man used to encase the dead in a crust of clay; with the advances of civilisation the clay crust developed into an urn or crock. In some cults the crust or covering for the dead was often a basket of rushes or willow. In Europe the basket was used for many hundreds of years. The victims of the guillotine in the French Revolution were rolled into baskets. The early Romans favoured stone coffins, preferably limestone, as did the Greeks before them. The word 'sarcophagus' is a Greek word meaning 'flesh eating' and it was believed that limestone eventually consumed the body, but other types of stone were frequently used. In England, stone coffins can be seen in the ruins of ancient abbeys and monasteries. It is said that each monk hewed his own coffin. Mahammed was buried in an iron coffin. Harvey, Physician to Charles I was 'lapped in lead'.

Since the earliest days of spinning and weaving, the dead were 'lapped' or 'wrapped' or 'wound' in cloth; winding sheets of linen or cotton were used in Egypt and in the whole of the Middle East. In England, during the middle ages, there was a law which stipulated that every corpse must be buried in a shroud of woollen cloth. This was a big help to the wool industry and might be quite a good law to introduce into New Zeland now when so much of the 1966 clip still awaits a market. The spinning and weaving of a 'funeral grey' cloth could help the farmer and the textile industry.

In 'How did it begin', R. Brasch writes 'Hundreds of years ago a "chested burial" was considered to be an attribute of the privileged classes'. The poor were conveyed from house to grave in what was termed a 'death-hamper' and there the corpse was removed and put in the grave wrapped in shroud or winding cloth, the hamper being retained for later use.

The word 'undertaker' as used today, is rather modern. It was first used of the person who presented and directed a pageant or a play. The funerals of kings were invested with pomp and pageantry and needed an 'undertaker'.

Gradually the term became 'funeral undertaker' and later gave place to the term 'funeral director'. It is still subject to change; in America there is a drift toward such elegant labels as 'grief therapist'. Long ago, only kings and a few very important people were given final resting place in church or church precincts. Landowners set aside an area for their dead, often within sight of their main windows. In some cases stone coffins were actually built into the dwelling itself. Unimportant people were buried with scant ceremony or discrimination in any convenient piece of ground, often quite close to the spot where the death took place. It became evident that proximity to a grave was sometimes unpleasant and so the dead were carried to a remote field. Thus our cemeteries came into existence and their formal name was 'The Necropolis' – 'city of the dead'. Cemetery is one of the 'escape' words; a euphemism which, at first, seemed less crude than necropolis, for its meaning was a 'sleeping place'. Now, cemetery is giving place to such American euphemisms as 'garden of memory'.

The tombstone was originally devised with a double purpose. Firstly, to prevent exhumation of the body by animals or evil doers, and secondly to prevent the dead from returning to torment the living. 'Resurrection of the dead' was not unknown when the 'dead' were deposited in caves or sepulchres: a coma, which sometimes supervenes an injury or very severe illness, could be mistaken for death.

The Australian writer, Alan Moorhead, says that the fear exhibited by the Aborigines when they first saw the white folk was due to the belief that their own dead ancestors were returning from their graves. Australian Aboriginal people are born pale and become pale when ill and after death. The pink skin of the Europeans seemed to them like the complexion of the long dead.

The early Christians were probably the only people who regarded temporary resurrection from the dead as a desirable thing. To most people, such a happening engendered more panic fear than welcoming delight. There is, however, one story of resurrection which is fraught with gentleness and love and not with fear or vengeance. It is a Japanese legend about the first Earth Mother who came back from the dead to see how her children fared and found them forlorn and sorrowful, so she went back to the country of the dead, but soon returned to the children bringing them a dog. Then she left them and rested content knowing that they would have a comforter and a friend forever.

The Egyptian practice of embalming the dead was the outcome of a belief in a physical survival after death; a belief not shared by Greeks or Romans but vigorously adopted by the early Christians. It might be asked why the Christians did not follow the Egyptian pattern still further and embalm their dead, since their belief in a physical resurrection was strong enough to make them defy the Roman law in regard to cremation. The answer is most probably that they were so convinced that the day of judgement was at hand, that to embalm seemed quite unnecessary. The ancient Egyptians little dreamed when they laid their embalmed loved ones to rest that some thousands of years later their dust would be prescribed as a medicine reputed to cure troubles such as plague or sterility. It is possible that any pretence of benefit derived from taking mummy-powder might be attributable to the balsam and other herbs, used lavishly in the embalming. Thousands of Egyptian mummies were consumed by Europeans in the middle ages; in fact, they ran out of mummies, and other dusts were fraudulently passed off as the genuine thing. There is no limit to humanity's ability to swallow queer prescriptions; one of the most revolting consisted of a brew of one fat puppy, a handful of earthworms, some turpentine and some oil of lilies, used as an ointment and as a precaution against Cholera and other epidemic evils.

Westgate (Parish Church in background) from an engraving by T. Kilby in 1853.

Chapter 9

Steel Pens and Influenza

1833

JANUARY 1st. There was snow on the ground this morning. We went to enquire about Eb who has been ill again and then called at Miss Stanilands. A lady called whilst we were there. I did not note her name, but noted that she spoke about having nine cats. When we got home Mrs. H. called and removed her bonnet without being invited to do so and we were most provoked. My aunt and uncle Wood called; aunt Wood is still not allowed to drink tea or coffee so we were obliged to serve beer for her.

January 7th. My cousins Jane, Eliza, Emma and Ellen called for us and we went together to Flanshaw. William and Mary Ann were already there when we arrived. We played cards as usual and all their talk was of the kind of men they intended to marry. The number of servants they could afford seemed to be the first consideration.

January 10th. Began making green fringe for my shawl. Maria Hausley called to ask me to drink tea with them this afternoon so I went at 5 o'clock. Mrs. Housley was not at home, she has been in London for the last four months visiting her daughter and son-in-law. Mr. Housley has just returned and had brought back two miniatures of his son and daughter which they had presented him with. They were drawn by Wilkie,[1] a very eminent artist and had cost 65 guineas each. Maria told me that her sister and brother-in-law had been painted life-size in their wedding clothes, her sister wearing all her jewellery of diamonds and pearls and that the same artist is now doing a portrait of the Princess Victoria. After I had seen and admired and commented, the miniatures were put away, but then

Mrs. H. and George arrived so there was a repetition of the whole recital and display. We had to admire and observe the fine clothes and the jewels and were told of the life size portraits which were costing 130 guineas each, and they talked of nothing but the style in which they live in London and about their great wealth. It seems to give the family immense delight. After all this we had some music and were very agreeable. Hannah came for me at 9 o'clock.

January 14th. At a musical evening at Miss Kettle's. We were in the upstairs drawing room. They sat Marion Housley down at the piano and as soon as she began to play they all began to talk. When she finished playing they asked me to play and I had exactly the same treatment. I am sure no one heard one note that either of us played. Later we joined the others downstairs and danced and I found it all rather dull.

January 18th. We had much company. We had taken up the drawing room carpet for dancing. Marion Housley looked quite queenly. Miss Fanny M. is now very tall and awkward but genteel in style. She was deranged some time ago due to her ungovernable passions and had to be confined in a private asylum: she is now quite better. We spent some time at first fortune-telling and looking at portfolios, then we danced about six sets of quadrilles, a country dance, the gallopades and then a waltz – the new dance. Everyone was most agreeable and we all danced famously until 11 o'clock.

January 19th. I felt very ill indeed today as I always do after much activity. I stayed in bed until 1 o'clock.

January 21st. Mrs. Scatcherd called and asked me to return with her to Morley for a short visit, but Mother would not permit it. I was much disappointed. Mother and Mrs. S. and I went to a bazaar at the White Hart. They both bought several things and I bought a steel pen[2] and shall write my journal with it in future.

February 3rd. Sunday. Sat in my uncle John's pew with cousin Ann as there was a lady sitting in ours. Ann slept during the sermon. Eb called and drank tea with us. She is very friendly now with a Mrs. Thomson, a widow, who has two grown-up sons and she lives in Westgate. These sudden friendships of Eb's never last very long.

February 6th. Mother and I went to see the foundation stone being laid of the new Proprietary School. Hustings had been set up for the ladies and we had very good seats. Mrs. Burton and Eb sat with us. There was a procession of the Freemasons and the Earl of Mexborough, the Provincial Master, laid the first stone. Prayers were said by Dr. Taylor. It was all over quite quickly and we played whist with Mrs. Burton and Eb when we returned home.

February 8th. Reading the life of Lord Byron. A Mr. B. called who is an executor of a person to whom my dear father mortgaged some property and this man wants Mother to pay off the mortgage. I was in the room and heard all the conversation. Mother told him that until Alfred comes of age, nothing can be settled and that she would consult Mr. Lumb about it. I cannot help feeling very grieved and fearful lest further misfortune befall us. Oh Almighty God, order everything for the best and save us from distress. Amen.

February 9th. Mother consulted her solicitor (Mr. Lumb) who says we must not be anxious about Mr. B. for until Alfred is 21 nothing can be done and that the property is entailed and so it is not in danger. Still I cannot help feeling disturbed.

February 12th. Went awalking with Eb as far as Snow Hill Bar. It was a lovely day, we met two of the Miss Lumbs there.

February 19th. Sewing in the morning. Went to Mr. Burton's soon after 2 o'clock. Eb and I went on the Ings and on to Alverthorpe, past the church and through Silcoates and Potovens and came on by Snow Hill. It was Shrove Tuesday and all the children were playing in the villages and the lads and young men playing cricket on the greens. It was a most beautiful day giving us a foretaste of spring.

February 20th. Reading Chamber's Edinbro Journal which I must return to the library. We went to my Uncle John's for dinner. Grandmother was there and Mary Ann, Jane and Alfred. We played several pools of quadrille in the dining room. Mary Ann and Jane teased Alfred a good deal and they quarrelled about counters and threw their cards at each other. It was with great difficulty that I restored peace. Later, we played whist and they became friendly again. It really is all Jane's fault; sometimes, I feel tired to death of card playing.

February 24th. Sunday. Went to Chapel. Miss Kendall was there and she came to talk to me and asked me to help with the Sunday school. She said my cousin Ann was going to do so and that she thought perhaps Ann had been trying to persuade me to help. I said she had never mentioned it but that I was very willing to help if I could. I do believe she was disappointed at my readiness.

February 26th. Alfred is much more attentive to Eb than he used to be. They sing duets together and I am sure Eb encourages him just to flatter her vanity. I am sure Alfred is not thinking of her seriously and after all she is so much older than he. I shall contrive to point that out to her sometime.

February 28th. I had a letter from Ellen Bayley, informing us that dear Mrs. Benjamin has had an operation last Friday for the removal of a cancer of the breast.[3] She is now as well as can be expected.

March 4th. Walked with Eb to Dirtcar and gathered beautiful Irish moss by the river. We walked back through Thornes Park. When we got home Mrs. Cummings called and we played whist. Mrs. Kendall called too, to ask Mother to subscribe to the Sunday school. She gave her 5/-.

March 5th. Went to my Uncle John's. Ann and Jane M. were there. Ann told me that Ann L. is going to marry a Mr. P. I was very surprised, he is said to be of genteel family, but he is a sad drunkard and card player and he is almost twice her age and prodigiously fat.

March 6th. Took the newspaper to my Uncle Wood and called at Mr. Barff's and then on Miss Stanilands to invite them to come to drink tea tomorrow. Miss P. was there. I went to school with her and used to be quite friendly. I can't understand what ever I saw to like. She is immensely tall and thin – so thin, that the flesh scarcely covers the bones. She has a pretty babyish face, very pale and dark hair worn in tight curls close to her head and no more animation than a statue. She is very deaf too.

March 19th. Sunday and I felt too ill to go to Chapel or Sunday school because of the toothache, so I decided to have my tooth out. I sent Hannah to fetch Kirkham (the dentist) and sat myself down, screwing up all my courage. Hannah held my head and Kirkham pulled the tooth half out an then it broke. He made several more attempts and broke all the top off it. He then had to probe with another instrument till he got the prongs out. It took quite 30 minutes and he must have made twenty attempts. Hannah became faint and sick and Alfred had to take her place holding my head and he was almost sick too. The dentist praised my courage and said he had never found a tooth so difficult to draw before. It was horribly painful and my gums bled till 11 o'clock at night and my face was much swollen and bruised.

April 2nd. Went to my Uncle Wood's. Miss Elizabeth Charlesworth was there; she is very delicate and they fear she is in a consumption.

April 6th. Cousin Ann and I went to several houses to enquire why their children had not attended Chapel and Sunday school. The people seemed quite glad to see us and were very civil indeed.

April 9th. Mr. Marsden (an attorney) and Mr. George Downing, the Master of Alverthorpe Work House called to ask Alfred to search amongst father's papers for some indentures which were more than 40 years old. They said they did not expect Alfred to find them, but if he did not, they would send him a subpoena to attend Pontefract Sessions to swear that he had made all possible search. It was to decide a case of settlement between Alverthorpe and

Wakefield. Alfred began the search at once but found no such record.

April 13th. Alfred returned from Pontefract where he has spent 2 days. He was not actually called to give evidence. He stopped with Mr. Hurst as he did not like the idea of the inn where they were sleeping four in a room. He seems to have enjoyed the outing and was well pleased with the expenses and hospitality allowances made to him. William Johnstone told Alfred that the Trustees at the Chapel have asked his father to give up half his income and have someone to do half the work. His father was so offended that he has resigned. The Johnstone family blame my uncle John very much for this as he is Chairman of the Trustees.

April 27th. We went to Alverthorpe. Henry had a very bad cold and looked very ill indeed. John spent the time trying to persuade me to make up my mind to marry. He says I should accept the very next offer because after 21 the offers become less frequent. I was much provoked by him. Just because he is himself engaged to be married very soon he thinks he can advise everyone else. He says he would come to our Chapel sometimes if he might use our pew and if we did not have such long sermons!

April 29th. Cousin Benjamin came to breakfast. He says Mrs. B. is much better and has been visiting her uncle at Crook Hill Hall but she cannot write yet because of pain in her arm resulting from the cancer operation.

May 1st. Eb called but she seemed very low spirited and not very well. She took wine and bread and butter and did not stop very long. The influenza is very prevalent at present, some person in almost every family has it and very often the whole family. My grandmother called on her way from town and we walked part of the way home with her. We left her at Humble Jumble and came back along Alverthorpe Lane. Mr. Scatcherd called and he gave Alfred some seeds of the orange gourd – a new and very beautiful plant. Mr. Scatcherd has just bought a cabinet to display his collection of coins.

May 5th. Sunday. Chapel and Sunday school. After today there will be evening service instead of afternoon. Ann was not there as she has got the influenza. By evening I felt very poorly with a very bad headache and coughing and vomiting – all symptoms of the influenza. I was obliged to go to bed and was very ill all night.

May 6th. Very ill all day.

May 7th. I sat up, wrapped in a blanket whilst my bed was made, but much the same as yesterday; very poorly. Mother is getting it now and is obliged to go to bed.

May 8th. Today Alfred is ill and now we are all very ill indeed.

May 9th. Hannah began to be ill and was obliged to stay in bed. I felt a little better. There was no one to admit Mrs. Swales (the woman who comes daily to do the rough work for Hannah) so she went away again which was a pity as she could have been a help to us.

May 10th. My aunt Wood called but she did not come upstairs. She just stood in the hall and called out to us. She did not offer to send any of her servants to help us, as I know she has done to some of her friends recently. I might have caught my death struggling up and down the stairs and into the cellars.[4] These were sad days for us all.

May 11th. Eb's father came. Hannah was much better and able to prepare some food for us. Mr. B. went into town and brought back crabs, which we ate and felt better. We had nothing except tea or coffee for several days. Miss Lindly called and just after she left my dear Mother fainted. We are all so very weak.

May 12th. Alfred went to the office today although he is not quite recovered. Captain D. and John called; they had been here several times to enquire about us.

May 15th. Today is Alfred's twentieth birthday.

May 16th. Called at my uncle John's. Most of them are well again except uncle John who is still in bed. I walked in the garden with Ann and we talked about our Sunday school scholars. Ann has two blackbirds which she strokes and kisses all the time. Mother and I then went to my grandmother's who has had the influenza too.

May 26th. Whitsunday and a lovely hot sunny day. Mr. Cannon preached for fifty minutes on the text 'take my yoke upon you'. We all liked it very much and never felt it the least bit too long. Mr. Cannon overtook us as we were coming home and we walked in the garden together for a short time. Eb came to drink tea and we sat in the garden until quite late.

May 28th. Mrs. Scatcherd sent to ask us to go to Morley this week but Mother sent word that we could not go till next week.

May 29th. Mother and I went to see the fashions at Miss Taylor's. There were very few things which I liked. Mother is having a black lace cloak made there. I went to visit Eb and helped her to sew shirts for Henry who is going next week to take up an appointment with a wool firm in Warwick. I stitched two cuffs and a collar.

[1] David Wilkie R.A. was one of the most highly esteemed artists of his time. He was appointed painter in ordinary to the King in 1830 and in 1837 was knighted by William IV. In addition to portrait painting he depicted scenes from everyday life, and in his later years did historical compositions. He is best known today by the former. His subjects are less sordid than those of Hogarth and other Georgian artists and the wealth of detail in his drawing provides an invaluable record of the dress and domestic conditions of that period. There is an engraving of 'The Blind Fiddler' hanging in the room in which I write, which never fails to fascinate. It depicts 12 people and a dog, in a room which might be the kitchen of a small farm. Three generations are gathered listening to the blind fiddler who sits in a high-backed chair. There are two chairs in the room, and by the big fireplace is a small cupboard which is open to display one wine glass, a bottle and a decanter, so this is no pauper family. All are warmly clad in voluminous garments and even the children wear shoes. They appear to be of the 'straight' type, i.e., no right or left foot, each shoe fitting either foot equally badly. A little girl is trailing a woollen yarn from a spindle and there are many signs of wool carding and spinning about the room. There are spades too and other signs of agricultural pursuits. A small boy, who is quite unlike the other children, is mimicking the fiddler, using for his violin and bow a fire bellows and a poker. The coarse face and style of this small boy would seem more at home in a Hogarth composition: was he a Parish orphan? The rest of the family are a comely group, only this boy is grotesque. The dog in the foreground looks as if he were a reformed bull-baiter, now old and amiable and battle scarred. One needs to remind oneself that sewing machines were not in use before 1840 and that every stitch in those garments was done by hand and the cloth home-spun and woven. It is also possible that most of the clothes worn were second-hand – handed down from father to son, from mother to daughter, from older to younger children or even bought from a second-hand

shop. Old clothes women made regular rounds of the better houses buying up cast-offs for resale to the poor. The garments of the dead often found their way to these mean shops and no doubt carried their quota of assorted germs to the new owners.

[2] Clara was remarkably early in the adoption of a steel pen. Longfellow changed in 1839, Matthew Arnold and Thomas Carlisle used the quill for another 20 years. In 1878 Fitzgerald complained bitterly at being obliged to use an 'iron' pen, so few quills being then available. It is quite obvious that the change-over was not made without some difficulties. For several pages after this entry the writing looks uncertain, scratchy and slightly blotchy. On settling down, the script becomes less flowing and more angular but decidedly easier to read and the ink is quite definitely less faded.

[3] This operation was performed about ten years prior to the introduction of general anaesthetics. The only pain killers then were liberal helpings of intoxicants such as brandy, rum or gin. Sometimes packs of ice and salt were applied to deaden skin sensitivitity.

[4] Indoor sanitary arrangements were not usual at that date but if any existed they were situated in cellars.

Chapter 10

Toll Bars and the Letters of Junius

JUNE 4th. My cousin the 'Rev' Thomas called and asked Mother to lend him our bible so that the Commissioners, who are sitting at the White Hart might see in what year poor Harriet Ellery was born.[1] Mother refused to lend it to him but told him he could take a copy, just as my uncle John had done – so he went away and came back to say that the Commissioner would not accept a copy but must see the Bible for themselves and asked if he might bring it to them if only for half an hour. But Mother still refused to let him take the book, but agreed to take it herself. So Hannah carried the Bible and Mother went with Thomas and showed it to the Commissioners and when they had read it she brought it back home. Thomas was not very pleased, in fact, I thought he seemed rather offended.

June 5th. Mother and I went by coach to Morley and it was so crowded that I was obliged to travel backwards until we got to Bingley Bar,[2] and there we had to pay 2/6 each to pass, which we thought quite exhorbitant. Arriving at Morley we found everyone well. Sarah Ann and I sat a long time together upstairs, she, telling me all the news – Mr. C. is paying his addresses to a 'twenty thousand pound heiress'; Miss C. has had an offer from Mr. B. but has refused him.

June 6th. Mother and Mrs. S. and I went to call on Mrs. Swinden and then on to call on Mrs. John Webster who is poorly and very lame now and they fear she is in a consumption. Mary played the piano for us and she plays very well indeed, after learning for only a year. A Mr. Thomas was there. He is an old bachelor of about 36 and they say he is going to marry a quite young lady.

June 7th. Mary had her music lesson in the morning. Mr. Hurst teaches her and he is a well known composer. Later we called on Mrs. Crowther and on returning several friends called to drink tea. It was all rather dull and very formal.

June 8th. Returned home. Mrs. S. and Mary promising to visit us in a fortnights time. I went to my Uncle Wood's; my aunt is in Harrogate with Mrs. Barff. Old Mr. Barff is very ill and not expected to recover.

June 9th. Sunday. Went to Chapel and Sunday School. A Mr. Turner of Halifax preached.

June 14th. Called to tell Miss Williamson to come to sew next week and then to Mrs. W. to enquire after her daughter who has just had her first baby. Mrs. Burton and Eb and Miss Colbeck called soon after I returned and we played at Giraffe in the garden and Alfred joined us and we all romped famously and then we played whist and sat in the garden until quite late. Miss Colbeck is about 19 and has a good figure but a very plain face.

June 18th. Busy helping Miss Williamson who is making a muslin gown for Mother. Alfred was away all day and did not come home till 7 o'clock, then after supper he said he had to go to meet William Johnstone at the office and he did not return till after 12 o'clock. Mother got into a perfect passion and fancied all the most unlikely things about him. She said she felt sure he had gone after no good and that he cared nothing for her or for me. I pacified her as well as I could and assured her that he was with William at the office and it was with great difficulty that I prevented her from setting off to find him. When he got home she was very angry and the poor lad was quite distressed for he really had had a very busy day and had really been with William.

June 27th. Cousin Ann and I went to call on my cousin Lawrance. Mrs. L. is expecting to be confined any day now. There are already two children and the eldest is terribly spoiled. Lawrance is so changed; he just lives for his family and thinks of little else. As we came home Ann bought a young swallow from a boy in the street. She has five birds already and this will be the sixth. She has also two dogs.

June 30th. Sunday. Went to the Sunday school and taught the scholars, my own, and Mrs. Holdsworth's too as she is away from home. Mrs. Heald went with me to Chapel in the evening and Mr. Cannon preached about the Calvinists and Mrs. Heald was very cross.

July 5th. The Fair Day. Mother and Mrs. S. went to the New Wells and into town to do some shopping and I stayed with Mary and dressed a little doll for her. Eliza Wood called; she says that her uncle Samuel has come over alone as his wife could not cross the Alps,[3] she is enceinte so he left her with friends at Bologna.

July 12th. Today is my dear Mother's birthday. May God grant her many very happy returns. Am reading more 'Fashionable Tales' by Miss Edgeworth which I like very much. Mr. and Mrs. Scatcherd and Samuel dined with us. Mother and Mrs. Scatcherd went shopping. Mr. Scatcherd told me they are thinking of sending Mary to a boarding school and Mary is delighted by the idea. Fanny is deafer than ever now and they have to shout at her.

July 24th. Sunday. I had 12 scholars today at the Sunday school – almost more than I could manage. My Aunt and Uncle Wood and the Dawsons dined with us and we were very merry. Captain and Mrs. D. teased Aunt Wood about her having five daughters to find husbands for. Aunt Wood is not used to being teased and I feared she might not be pleased but she was not at all vexed and we all laughed incessantly. They lectured dear Mother, saying that she must really have me christened in a church so that I might procure a register. They said Henry could perform the ceremony one day soon and Captain D. and my aunt Wood could be my god-parents and then we should all meet for a fine dinner party to celebrate. It was all quite good-natured nonsense.

July 25th. My Uncle Wood came to tell us that Johnathan Scott died yesterday of the Cholera. We were very much shocked. He was here at our house on Saturday morning last. There are several other cases reported in the town. Samuel Barff is leaving tomorrow for Bologna, he is anxious to rejoin his wife there. I am reading 'Emma' and like it very much.

July 26th. Eb came to breakfast and to our surprise her brother Henry called at about 11 o'clock with Horatio Ogden from St. Ives, so Eb went home with them. I went to the library to get more of Miss Edgeworth's 'Fashionable Tales' and later Jane and Elizabeth and I walked to Lowe Hill. It was a lovely clear evening and the view was beautiful but there were such queer looking men[4] there that we were afraid and walked quickly along to the bridge at Dirtcar. There we were overtaken by Mr. C. in his gig and we stopped to talk for a while with him. They always tease me about him and say he is madly in love with me – just nonsense of course.

July 28th. Sunday. Chapel and Sunday school. A Mr. Higgins from Hull preached. I did not admire his style, too theatrical. After Chapel we went to Flanshaw and found the heat most oppressive; there was not a breath of air. No one could talk of anything but poor Jonathan Scott. We went to Chapel again in the evening: I love evening service, it is so quiet and the sun-shine gives the Chapel a mellow and holy look.

August 4th. Sunday. Mr. Cannon preached refuting the doctrine of original sin. It is very cold today and after the recent great heat we all feel it very much. Marian Housley called in the evening to bid us goodbye, she is going to her sister in London to spend winter. Yesterday Alfred and William Johnstone went to Leeds to see an exhibition of pictures and they met Mr. and Mrs. Scatcherd and Watson there. Watson is at school in Leeds and Samuel is now a boarder at Mr. Williamson's of Gomersal. Watson goes to the Leeds Grammar School but lodges with a Mr. Haworth.

August 13th. Mr. and Mrs. Scatcherd came and we drove back with them to Morley. The family are all well but poor Fanny is as deaf as a post. She has been taking something recommended by a physician in Leeds but it has made her worse. It is most unfortunate; she is a nice child and quite pretty too.

August 14th. It was so wet we had to stay indoors. I read the 'Gentleman's Magazine' and Mary did her practice on the piano. In the afternoon we drove over to Leeds to see the exhibition of pictures and saw Watson at his school.

August 15th. Drove to Gomersal to see Samuel, who seems tolerably comfortable with Mr. and Mrs. W. They are Scotch people. He is a Calvinist Minister (but formerly was in the Church). I observe that Mrs. Scatcherd is definitely enceinte.

August 17th. Mr and Mrs. Swinden came to drink tea. Mr. Swinden has just published another book. It is to prove that Chatham was actually 'Junius',[5] and that the miscellaneous letters were spurious. The conversation was mostly on that subject and on the new unions of the working people, throw-outs and such things.

August 19th. We went to dine at the Swinden's. The Websters were there and Mr. and Mrs. Hill and Mr. Cassel who made a great fuss of me. We looked at some Hogarth prints and other prints in a very large album. I am sure my cousins Jane and Mary Ann would really love Mr. Cassel. He has such contempt for dependants and vulgar people.

August 20th. Returned to Wakefield. James driving us over in the gig. We went along to my uncle Wood's. They have all gone into black for poor Elizabeth Charlesworth who died last week.

August 25th. Sunday. Chapel and Sunday school and the scholars really do improve though Ann Speight told me today that the greatest of all the Commandments was to love ourselves as well as ever we could! A young man from Manchester preached. After the sermon Mr. Cannon got up and said he had had an anonymous letter last week attacking his principles and he begged the writer, if present, to meet him after the service in the vestry or in his own home in order that he might answer him.

August 30th. Went to visit Eb. We played cards as usual and Mr. B. was drinking and smoking as usual in the dining room. They sent Emma (a maid) to ask Mother if I might stay to drink tea with them.

September 2nd. Alverthorpe Races. We went with my cousins to visit Grandmother who had provided a great meal and most of them ate as if it were the most important thing in life. Cold meats and pies of all kinds. We played whist and everyone was very merry. We saw the Alverthorpe Sunday school scholars 'walk' – they came through the Fold as we were going on to Flanshaw.

September 3rd. Henry Burton is back home. His appointment did not last long. Poor Eb has many troubles. I ought to be thankful that I have a brother like Alfred. Old Mr. Barff died last night. Mrs. H. called, she told us that Hannah is going to a finishing school. I think it should be a 'beginning' school as the poor child has had little education up to now and she is 15 years old.

September 6th. I called at my Uncle Wood's. Mary Ann told me she had seen her grandfather soon after he died and was so shocked by his appearance that she had fainted and then had gone into hysterics. Then I called to see Eb who says Henry is going to begin business (wool) for himself as soon as he is of age, which will be next month.

September 14th. Mother and Alfred and I went to Alverthorpe Hall. The conversation as I had expected was about the Rev. E.R. – a lecturer who was so renowned for his sanctity that he even refused to visit Unitarians[6] whom he thinks wicked. He has been deprived of his parish and his lectureship and his place as Chaplain at the prison and is leaving Wakefield. The Dawsons say it is a heavy penalty for such a 'trifling and natural offence' as the Rev. Henry calls it. I felt so provoked that I think I shall never visit there again. I felt my face constantly blushing.

September 15th. Sunday. We gave each of our scholars a tract as a reward for good conduct. I have become quite fond of my class and one child in particular; a little girl of eight called Emma Marriott.

September 16th. Reading a book by Mrs. Trollope. Mother and I called on Mrs. Burton. Eb has got some goldfish and gave me two silver ones and lent me a glass dish to keep them in. We called at Lockwood's and bought 4 yards of Irish cloth[7] for Alfred to paste his plans upon.

September 20th. Mr. and Mrs. S. and Watson and Samuel came to dine. Watson had the toothache all day. Mother and Mrs. S. went shopping and Mrs. S. bought a carpet and squirrel tippets for Mary and Fanny.

September 22nd. Sunday. Sunday school at 9.30. I asked Eliza Robinson the meaning of the word 'authority' and she said 'it is to be a missis over somebody' – well, she had the correct idea. We had evening service for the last time this year. After today it will be in the afternoon. Mr. Cannon preached an old sermon, but it was a good one.

September 26th. Eb and I walked to Lowe Hill and it was a most delightful day, clear and pleasant. We bent our heads down and then looked up from the hill, and it had a very curious effect. We walked on to Dirtcar and stood for a long time looking at the Danestakes. On the way home we bought cheese cakes at a cottage and I went back with Eb to drink tea. Her father was drinking and smoking as usual in the dining room.

[1] There was at this time, no compulsory notification of Births, Deaths or Marriages. Such official records as existed were those kept by the Established Church, but entries in family bibles were accepted as legal evidence in the Courts. The importance given in years gone by to parental consent to a marriage is well understood, for non-approval meant no record of the marriage in the family Bible or on the pedigree.

[2] The toll bar and turnpike system revolutionised the roads of England. The Romans had been great road builders, but after they left Britain there was no longer any overall plan or control. The upkeep of roads fell on the villages or farmlands through which they passed and the labour was forced labour and therefore bad and amateurish. The tollgate system promoted the idea of 'the user pays' and road-making and maintenance became a business for experts. The system was first introduced in the reign of Queen Anne but in a very limited way. The tremendous trade development of the early 19th Century made better roads imperative and the Toll Bars were the means by which this improvement was achieved. By the year 1840 there were 8,000 such bars in England and the roads were reasonably safe and usable all the year round. Before this era, travelling even short distances was an adventure not to be lightly entered upon. In the winter months the roads were so muddy that they were impassable

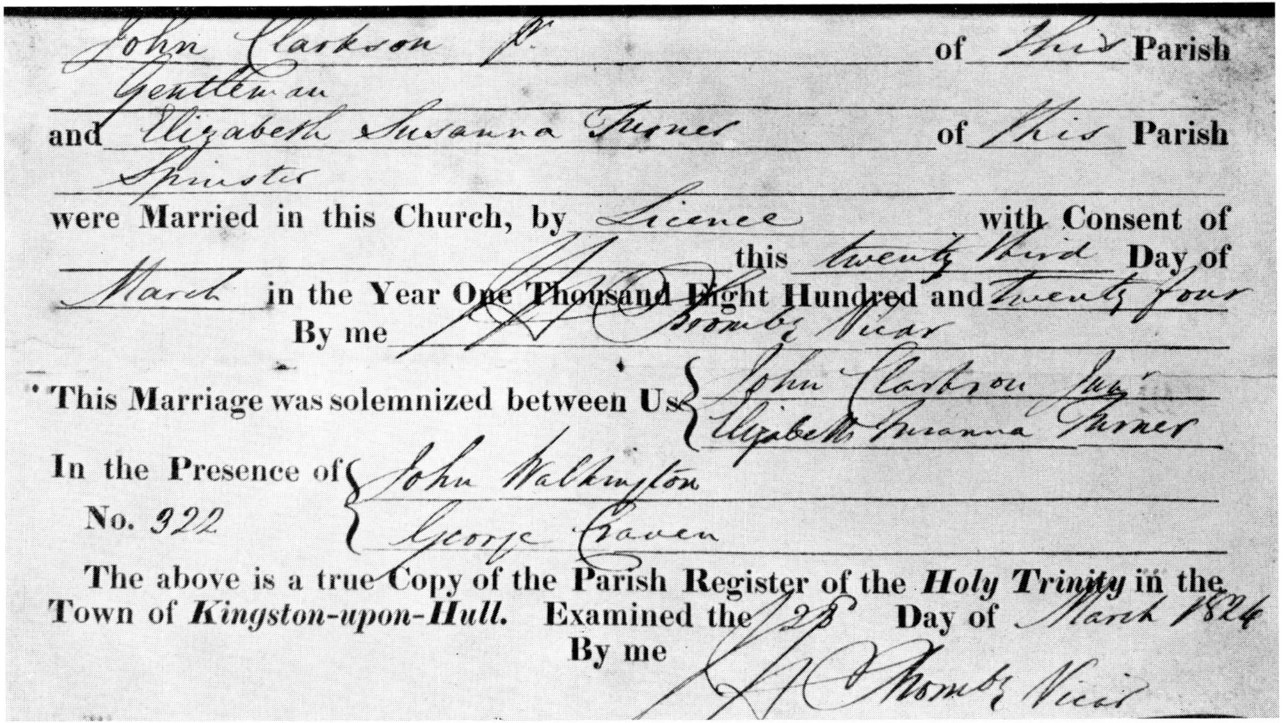
John Clarkson Jr. of This Parish
Gentleman
and Elizabeth Susanna Turner of This Parish
Spinster
were Married in this Church, by Licence with Consent of
this twenty third Day of
March in the Year One Thousand Eight Hundred and twenty four
By me [illegible] Bromby Vicar
This Marriage was solemnized between Us { John Clarkson Junr. / Elizabeth Susanna Turner }
In the Presence of { John Walkington / George Craven }
No. 322
The above is a true Copy of the Parish Register of the *Holy Trinity* in the Town of *Kingston-upon-Hull.* Examined the 23 Day of March 1824
By me [illegible] Bromby Vicar

C. of E. Marriage Lines, 1824 – before the introduction of State Registration.

for wheeled vehicles. Pack mules were used for transport of goods in areas not serviced by canals or rivers. The private traveller went on horseback or on foot. In spring a road plough or grader drawn by eight horses was used to clear the roads and after that, waggon-teams had right of way over coaches and private travellers. Meat for the city dwellers was brought to town 'on the hoof'. In spring and summer the roads were cluttered with cattle, sheep, geese and turkeys which added to the general confusion, filth and inconvenience of the traveller. The grassy hedgerows provided grazing for the slow-moving livestock and also gave good shelter to the highwaymen who were an everpresent menace to road users.

Turnpike roads were sealed and in widening the carriage-way, much of the shelter for highwaymen was eradicated. Another benefit of the system was the opening up of back country. Tax-evaders made by-paths which eventually developed into side-roads which added to travelling comfort considerably. Apart from the elegant and important carriages which required two or four horses and a couple of grooms, the 'run-about' of those days was the 'gig' and it was very unlike the light, speedy, rubber-shod two-wheeled trap which many of us can remember and which still cuts a dash in the Grand Parades at our Agricultural Shows. It was at that time a ponderous body of great weight fixed high upon iron-clad wheels with two enormous bow springs at the rear and an immense adjustable hood. With a good strong horse and a following wind on a good road it could do about four miles an hour, but roads were not very good and accidents were frequent.

Horseback continued to be the most mobile and speedy mode of travel throughout the 19th Century and the many Bridle Paths of England still provide for those few who tread them the most charming glimpses of an England inaccessible to the motorist.

[3] Crossing the Alps by the St Gotthard Pass was done in those days mostly on mules. Between 1820 and 1830 a carriage road was built but it was a dangerous road and there were frequent avalanches. The Hospice at the summit had been destroyed by French soldiers and was not rebuilt until 1834, so that the journey was not ideal for an expectant mother.

[4] The moors around Wakefield and between Keighley and Huddersfield were popular meeting places for Luddites and Chartists. Since the Chartist marches in 1830 there had been few major demonstrations. The workers at that time were demanding a wage of half-a-crown a day. Three of their leaders were hanged and more than 400 workers were deported to Australia. The passing of the Reform Bill and the elections of 1832 had had a calming effect on the masses but the smouldering discontent was still there and a great underground movement was being organised by the Chartists.

[5] This mention of Junius is an interesting reference to the troubled days of the seventeen sixties and the squabbles between Parliament and Wilkes and the reformers. The identity of 'Junius' had never been established, but publishers of the so-called 'miscellaneous letters' were prosecuted. At least forty persons were at various times pronounced to be the authors of the letters criticising the King, Parliament and its foreign policy. The most often mentioned was the Duke of Bedford (a former Prime Minister), the Duke of Grafton and Lord Mansfield but the hot favourite was Sir Philip Francis. Ten or a dozen books have been written attributing authorship to various people; one was published as recently as 1927 purporting to prove that Lord Shelburne was the writer. Mr. Swinden's contention that Chatham was the author was as good a guess as any. Chatham (Pitt the Elder) was twice Prime Minister. He had very bad health and in his many periods of enforced retirement could have devoted much time to letter writing. The letters were elegant in style and written with a great fund of background knowledge. He was reported to have told many people that he knew the name of the writer and that it was definitely not Sir Philip Francis. However, it is pointed out in the *Encyclopaedia Britannica* that

'many a man has been hanged on less evidence than that presented in the case of Sir Philip'. It is one of those old historical puzzles which may never be solved. Certain it is that Chatham was a supporter of Wilkes and a reformer at heart. An Earldom, conferred in 1766 put curbs on him and lost him many friends but his genius has never been questioned and his foreign policies were sound.

[6] In the time of Shakespeare, Unitarians were burned as heretics. However, in 1677 a law was passed which abolished the death penalty for heresy. The Bill of Rights and the Act of Toleration of 1689 excluded Unitarians because of their non-acceptance of the doctrine of the Trinity. The embargo gradually relaxed though the High Church never softened its stern views in regard to such unbelievers.

[7] Linen was so called; woollen cloth was called 'English cloth'.

Chapter 11

Historic Place Names

WAKEFIELD was the centre of a well settled area long before the Romans set foot in Britain. It was here that the Wake plays and fairs were held in Neolithic days. Close by, was the defensive hill, the 'Caer', which was the Celtic word similar in meaning to the Roman 'Castra', a fort or strong point. In his book 'The English Heritage', R. W. Finn expresses the opinion that the many stone circles in Britain were not entirely of religious significance but that they were primarily defence areas in which the surrounding husbandmen with their families and flocks could take refuge during feudal wars or foreign invasion. The Caers were perhaps of slightly later date than the stone circles and were hill sites strengthened by water courses, great dykes specially constructed and sometimes diverted rivers. They gave shelter and security, just as the stone circles had done and were easier to defend. Dirtcar is a corruption of Ditcaer – a 'caer' or fort, strengthened by a ditch or 'Dit'.

Lowe or Lawe Hill is very close to the village of Dirtcar and Lowe or Lawe was the ancient name for a hill. In his memoirs, Henry Clarkson wrote 'Lawe Hill was a contested place between Wakefield and Thornes. On public holidays such as Easter Monday and Whitsuntide it was a regular battle-field, the contest being sharply waged between Thornes and Wakefield lads. Stones were freely used by the combatants and the victorious party would chase their fleeing foes into Thornes or the confines of Wakefield, as the case might be. I have joined these mimic battles with my school fellows, the Holdsworths and the Burrells and given and received many an awkward blow'. It is a very safe assumption that these 'mimic battles' were held in commemoration of the old grim fights for supremacy fought periodically on this site for over 2,000 years and it is also very probable that the hill now called 'Lowe Hill' was the original site of Ditcaer – the entrenched hill fort, and that a village which subsequently grew up in its vicinity took for itself the name of the historic Mount. Potovens, another nearby village, must have been the area set aside for cooking operations. Pot or pitovens were the cooking ovens of the Neolithic age. Specimens have been found around Stonehenge and other ancient centres of population and were no doubt used in connection with the great gatherings held in and around the strong-point or Caer and in the Wake fields nearby. The pot-ovens seem to have been very similar to the Maori ovens with which we are so familiar in New Zealand. Holes or pits were dug and lined with stones; other larger stones were heated in nearby fires and rolled into the pots or pits where the meats to be cooked had been placed. This was done in layers until the pit was full and then the top was sealed with turf to keep in the steam and heat. They had no flax mats such as the Maori uses but were versed in the crafts of weaving and thatchery and no doubt mats of reed or rushes were used between the meats and the earth sods.

The Roman imprints on the area are represented by castles such as Pontefract and Sandal, but the Romans had no need for shelter over long periods for great numbers of men or flocks. All they required was safe lodgings for mobile troops between London and Edinbro'. The Danes made a much greater impression in many parts of Britain. This is shown especially in place names of Yorkshire and East Anglia. Denmark is a flattish land of gently rolling fertile farm lands and the Danes always settled in places as nearly like home as they could find. The number of towns and villages which end in 'by' are indicative of their origin for 'by' is Danish for 'place'. Thus we find Selby, Denby, Grimsby, Whitby and many more, and such endings as 'toft', 'thorp', 'garth' and 'kirk' are typically Danish; our word 'by-law' is a Danish relic meaning a local law or place law.

The Danes remained in Britain for about 300 years. They were good colonisers; they intermarried with the local people and lived at peace with them. When the Normans came, they put up as bitter a resistance as any. The so called 'Danes dikes' along the Yorkshire coast were there long before the Danes arrived, but they used them and maintained them as they used most of the ancient established strongpoints. An interesting light is shed by Finn on another feature frequently seen on hills in the British Isles – the stone cairns, generally believed to be ancient burial sites. Finn writes 'the cairns which decorate so many hillsides and hilltops sometimes owe their origin also to a custom. The clan marching out to battle each gathered one stone which was placed in a heap; after victory or defeat, each survivor abstracted a stone, the residue giving the number of slain and providing a memorial to the dead' – the earliest of all war memorials; perhaps the proverb 'dead men tell no tales' originated as 'dead men take no tallies', for tale and tally were the same word. Long before men learned to use written symbols for counting, stones or beads were universal usage. To 'tell beads' was to count by beads or pebbles – we still have bank 'tellers' who 'tell' or count the money paid in or out by the bank and Parliamentary tellers who count the votes after a 'division'.

The mention of Danestakes entailed much more research than most place names. There is no such word in any dictionary or book of reference which I have come across. It is possible that the name is a corruption of two very ancient words, the oldest being 'wapentakes'. In the dictionary of Phrase and Fable, Brewer writes: 'a wapentake was a division of Yorkshire similar to that better known as a "hundred". The word means "touch arms", it being the custom of each vassal, when attending the assemblies of the district, to touch the spear of his overlord in token of homage'. Wap or whop means tap, stroke or beat as in 'whip-ma-whap-ma gate' in York where malefactors were flogged or whipped. The word 'take' came to refer to the actual area over which the vassal secured tenure by the gesture of homage. When the Danes came they could not expect this gesture of allegiance from the local lordlings. What they did exact was not a gesture but a tangible tribute of coin or kind which became known as the Danesgeld. When the Normans arrived in 1066 they were quite delighted by this custom. It was their first encounter with anything resembling an income tax and they cherished the idea. It is very possible that the landscape referred to as 'Danestakes' were the takes or holdings from which the Danes had exacted their 'geld'. So Danestakes has come about as a complex corruption of two words – Wopentake and Danesgeld. The word wopentake is peculiar to Yorkshire and is very infrequently encountered even there. It is quite possible that the existence of Danesgeld was the inspiration of the Domesday book.

The Domesday book was certainly compiled largely with taxation in mind. Records were made of land ownership and its potentialities and an assessment of tribute or tax decided upon, usually a tithe to be paid in kind and these records were known as 'tallies' from 'tale', meaning a count or a history. These records were made on rods of wood, notched or marked and then split lengthwise, the Exchequer keeping one half and the tax payer the other. When the tax was paid there was a check made to show that the amount tallied with the state's record. These tallies were not discarded by the Exchequer until 1834 when, according to Brewer, two cartloads of them were burned at 6 o'clock in the morning and the operation was so ill managed that it started a fire in the Houses of Parliament and in part of the Palace of Westminster. The Domesday book itself was kept in a room in Winchester Cathedral called the 'Domus Dei', thus the word 'Domesday' evolved. No copies of the great book were made until 1783. It is now stored in the Record Office.

Flanshaw is another local historic site. The name means a clearing in a copse or woodland and it must have been a habitation in very ancient times. It is mentioned in the Domesday book and the fact is noted that a Druid's oak stands by the homestead. The house in which Clara's grandmother lived was built in the reign of Elizabeth the first. It was a low rambling place, built of small Elizabethan bricks and roofed with flags and lead. It had mullioned windows, oak panelled rooms and much original Elizabethan and Cromwellian furniture. It had been the scene of 'the sheltering of the Five Hundred' during the religious persecutions before the Pilgrim Fathers sailed for New England.

In the latter half of last century it had become dilapidated as the result of a subsidence and one wing was closed up and unused. The rest was divided into four dwellings – in New Zealand we would call them 'flats'. My father used to say that he would restore the place to its original state and live there, but by the time he inherited it, the cost of restoration and maintenance was well beyond his means and in 1919 he sold the property. The Hall was bought by some Americans. It was dismantled, shipped and reconstructed somewhere in Maryland and a modern housing estate now occupies the old site.

Chapter 12

Sunday School Affairs

SEPTEMBER 28th. It is all arranged that Mr. Cannon is to have the Chapel, but till his health improves he can preach one sermon of his own composition each Sunday and read the other one and meanwhile we are to have students from York in turns. We were at my Uncle Wood's and Miss Stanilands was there and Miss Hardcastle. They were fortune telling. Miss Hardcastle firmly believes in it all, in planet-rulers and such things; rather a silly girl I think. All the conversation was about Mr. Patrick who came to Wakefield to settle Rushworth and Co's affairs [bankers who failed] and he has gone off with a great deal of money belonging to the creditors. He lived at St. Johns in very great style and the family was much respected.

October 1st. Reading 'Kenilworth' but had a very bad headache. Mr. Scatcherd is annoyed because uncle had bought, or ordered for him, shares in the new Proprietary school and he says he will not take up shares till he knows more about the plans and approves of them, so Alfred, who was going to Morley to take him some iris roots, will take him a prospectus and explain about it all. Captain D. and John called. They are very tiresome. They want Mother to do all kinds of renovations for them. She is having the whole place painted but they want her to have the glazing of the hot houses done and repair the iron railings by the gate, which she says they should do themselves.

October 2nd. Alfred was late coming home and Mother torments herself so about him. If he is the least bit late she always fancies he has gone to places he should not go to, yet I know and would risk my life that he would never do such a thing or anything else which is wrong. I am so sorry he is late simply because it makes Mother so uneasy and when she is so she says things she would not otherwise say. God Almighty, comfort her. Amen. We had a very bad night and neither of us slept.

October 3rd. At a party at Mrs. O'Dwyer's. There was a Mr. Dennis B. there, an old bachelor of about 45, and Mr. Cannon's brother was there too. He is an artist – a big vulgar looking fellow and quite different from our minister.

October 6th. Sunday. A student from York with a very silvery voice preached on the text 'If a man die, shall he live again'. I liked it very well.

October 14th. Mother and I went to Leeds with Mary Ann and Eliza. Mary Ann bought black jet ear-rings at a stall in the Central Market and the girl at the stall bored her ears for them. They bled a great deal and were very troublesome and I thought her very foolish to have them done so. We bought materials and silk stockings and Eliza bought a lynx boa and Mother went to arrange about a carpet and several other things. We were very tired by the time we arrived home.

October 15th. Mr. Cannon called and he asked if Alfred would help with the Sunday school.

October 19th. David B. came at half past six to tell us that my grandmother has had a paralytic stroke. We went at once to Flanshaw and found her better than we had expected, but she has lost the use of one side. We sent for Teal and had him make a bed for her downstairs and so we left her quite comfortable. On the way home we called at my Uncle Wood's to tell them about grandmother and I am sure my Aunt Wood was quite glad to hear the bad news.

October 20th. Sunday. Mother and Alfred went quite early to Flanshaw and I to Sunday school. Mr. Holdsworth told me that Miss Kendall had turned four of her scholars away for wearing gloves[1] and another for going to a love-feast.[1] She has done this kind of thing before and we are all most provoked. She always fills their places with the best girls from other peoples classes and we may soon find ourselves with no scholars at all. We are considering what is best to be done. After school I went to Flanshaw and coming through Alverthorpe I could scarcely get along for people stopping to ask about grandmother.

October 27th. Sunday. Alfred took a class at Sunday school for the first time. He chose nine boys for a class of his own and I chose seven girls for a class of my own too. The eldest is about 8 and none of them can read so it will not be very easy.

October 28th. Went to see my grandmother who is not so well. She has had a second stroke and is very low spirited. The lane was very muddy and it was not easy walking.

November 2nd. I bought today some spelling books and a Child's History Book for my Sunday school scholars and covered them carefully with brown paper.

November 3rd. Sunday. Miss Kendall asked me to let her have three of my scholars for her class which is very small now but I did not agree to part with them.

November 6th. A very windy day. Coming home from my Uncle Woods my petticoats were almost blown over my head. Later in the day we went to Flanshaw and found grandmother very weak. We have a new sewing woman; a Miss Deckens. She has made a stuff gown and trimmed it nicely; it has a stomacher front.

November 16th. Eb has broken her goldfish bowl and cut her finger very badly. We are now sharing with Mr. B. in taking the Leeds Mercury instead of the Wakefield Star, which is not as good as it was when Nichols was the proprietor of it.

November 17th. Sunday. Took my own class at Sunday school. Went again in the afternoon and the preacher (a student from York) did not arrive till three o'clock and we were almost in the dark.

November 20th. We went to Mr. Burton's to celebrate Eb's 25th birthday. We played Whist. William seems to be fatter every time I see him. He really is quite fat enough for a side show at a Fair. Eb had a bad cold and toothache.

November 21st. Mother and I went to Lockwood's and I bought ribbons to trim my new bonnet. When we got home Mrs. Benjamin called to bid us goodbye. She is going back to Sheffield after visiting at Newmillerdam. She did not dismount; she is very fond of riding and so pleased to be able to do so again after her operation.

November 23rd. Very wet and windy. Cousin Ann came and stayed till 8 o'clock and Alfred was obliged to take her home. She talked all the time of Mr. Cannon, our new minister and borrowed the 'Elements of Botany' from Alfred and says she is going to apply herself to the study of it. I am sure it is just to attract Mr. C. I hear that dear Eb is quite poorly.

November 25th. I went to see Eb who has a swelling on her gum which is very painful and Mr. Bennett (the surgeon) was there and ordered three leeches to be put in her mouth.

December 2nd. My cousin Ann called, she wants to try on my new tiny bonnet. I am sure she is making a dead set at Mr. C. She is convinced he is as fond of animals as she is, and she always talks to him about them.

December 3rd. Went to Mrs. S. H.'s. There were several people there including my cousin Ann and Mr. Cannon. Mrs H. sent Hannah back to tell Mother that they were keeping me to take supper with them and that they would see me safely home. I was sure that Mother would be angry and felt most uneasy but what could I do? Mr. C. sang and I played his accompaniments. He said he would see me home and it was nearly half past eleven when we left. We met Hannah in York St., and I made Mr. Cannon leave us there and came on with Hannah, as I dared not let him come to the house lest Mother should scold him. Hannah told me that my mother had been out herself to meet me earlier. I am so glad we met Hannah and not my Mother. As soon as I arrived she began to scold me angrily in a way I shall never forget. I tried to tell her and explain but it was useless. Alfred was most upset to hear her speak to me so. It is so very seldom that I go anywhere without her and if

I do I cannot enjoy it. She always seems so angry and offended. It is not as if they had not sent word by Hannah and Mr. Cannon is our minister so she should not have been uneasy about me. I wept bitterly in bed.

December 4th. Mother did not speak to me all day, but I tried to talk to her and told her when I went out to visit Eb. When I came home she was still sulky and cross so I told her I thought I was the one with most reason to be upset and she said she would not have said so much had I not tried to contradict her, but I did not do so and Alfred said he knew I did not either. My eyes were aching with crying so much and I think Mother really was sorry about it but could not say so.

December 6th. Alfred went to supper at Mr. T.'s and did not come home till after eleven. I sat up for him.

December 11th. Last night was quite tempestuous, hail and rain, snow, thunder and lightening.

December 12th. Went to Flanshaw and found grandmother much better. She had taken a walk in the garden with the help of a stick. She really is wonderfully better, poor dear! As we came home we met Cap. D. and John, they were quite blue with the cold.

December 14th. Poor grandmother is very ill again. I went with my Aunt Wood and Elizabeth. We walked across the fields. It was cold and very windy and most unpleasant. Grandmother has lost the use of one side again. Elizabeth's bonnet blew away in the wind three times and it was quite spoilt.

December 15th. Sunday. Chapel and Sunday school. Today we sat with the scholars in the seats at the back of the Chapel and liked the new idea very well. We began also collecting money from the boys. We are to bank 6 pence for them for every 5 pence they save. We each have twelve boys to collect from.

December 18th. I went with cousin Ann to several of the houses to tell the mothers of the Sunday school scholars about the new savings bank plan. They were all most civil and said they were much obliged to us.

Christmas Day. We went to visit my grandmother who was a little better and more cheerful.

December 26th. My Uncle and Aunt Wood and the six children dined with us and two of their servants dined with Hannah. They were all very regretful that Alfred has not become fond of dancing. They are to give a dance quite soon and say that J.H. is to arrange it for them. They talked of nothing but fashions all evening and I was heartily glad when they left.

December 31st. There was a tremendous high wind and several people were blown over in the streets and knocked against walls and were much hurt.

[1] The wearing of gloves was as reprehensible as the wearing of a bonnet instead of a head shawl or cap. It was apeing their betters. What was meant by a 'love feast' is not so easily explained. I heard the expression used in the Chamber of a catacomb in Malta. The guide told us that in one of the large caves the early Christians celebrated their love-feasts. No one asked him what a 'love-feast' was and I concluded that I was the only one who did not know. However, it later transpired that none of the others knew, and everyone was asking everyone else but no one knew the answer. It could be an old-fashioned way of referring to the Communion Service.

Chapter 13

Storms, Prayers when Salting Pork

1834

JANUARY 1st. Two of the Flanshaw tenants came to tell us that their windows had been blown out and slates off. Cap. D. and John came to say that some trees had blown down and several slates from the stables. They were in a good mood. I hope the trees falling will not have disturbed the Rooks. It is supposed to bring bad luck if the Rooks forsake a property – whose luck would this be, ours or the Dawsons? Something like this happened many years ago and dear Father had the trees trimmed and nests made and placed in the branches to entice the Rooks to come back and they did so after a little while.

January 5th. Sunday. Chapel and Sunday school. Miss Alexander took a class today and I gave her one of my pupils. Mr. Cannon preached an excellent sermon, the text being 'Remember the days that are past'.

January 6th. Cousin Benjamin came to breakfast. He brought me some ivory toothpicks[1] which he makes very cleverly. He went on later to the Christening of the Rev. Thomas's child who is to be named Frances Benjamin Bayley Clarkson.

January 7th. Miss Dickinson is here altering a black silk gown for Mother and I helped during the morning. Eb came and she told me that Mr. Horner had preached at Thornes last Sunday. She says he comes to Thornes purposely to meet her. She used to like him I know before she became interested in John C. We had a long serious conversation about religion and I confess I feel rather envious of Eb. I did my best not to be jealous and prayed to God to forgive me and to bless Eb and make her happy.

January 10th. Alfred and I went to see the show of Wild Beasts, then on to visit Eb and Eb went with us to visit my grandmother and walked back home through Alverthorpe where we met John Dawson. The roads were very muddy after the heavy rains.

January 17th. It was quite a large dance at my cousin's. I never danced so much in one evening ever before and enjoyed it greatly.

January 18th. I felt quite ill in the morning and spat a great deal of blood as soon as I awoke. I have done this for several years now after any unusual exertion. Later in the day I went to the library and got 'Red Gauntlet'.

January 19th. Sunday. Chapel and Sunday school. Ann and I sat with the scholars in the side seats, in the morning, and Mrs. H. and her daughter now do the same in the afternoon.

January 21st. Dear Mother is much troubled by a scorbutic eruption.

January 23rd. Mr. Burton came to tell us that Henry and Mary Walker had been married at the Old Church about a week ago and they had heard only that day. I was not surprised. It was so windy today that it was not easy to stand or walk out of doors, but I went to my uncle John's. One of Ann's blackbirds is ill and they are all quite distressed about it. Cousin Henry came in whilst I was there. He says Mrs. H. is declared definitely enceinte. He is just like my uncle Wood, quite managed and mastered by his wife, but he is a very good son too, so his sister Ann assures me. Mother and I sat up waiting for Alfred till after 12 o'clock and when he had not come I persuaded her to go to bed and I sat up alone till he came at half-past-one. He said he had been at Mr. Walker's office with William Johnstone.

January 24th. Mr. Swinden came to give us news of Mrs. Scatcherd (who has a third son) she is now well and out again. This boy is to be called Oliver.

February 3rd. Mother said I might go to Sandal with cousin Ann tomorrow and stay the night. After supper I very stupidly and unthinkingly said something to provoke Mother and she scolded me violently and Alfred defended me which made Mother more angry and she told Alfred that she had always thought that he would 'be the death of her'. He was terribly hurt and after he went to his room I told Mother that she should not have spoken to him so, for she had no reason to and that indeed she had a great deal to be thankful for in having so good a son. She was very angry and said things to both of us that she did not believe herself. I told her how sorry I was for speaking as I had done and that I had not intended to offend her and begged her to forgive me and forget it. I wept bitterly in bed all night and made a strong resolution to keep a strict guard on my tongue in future and prayed more earnestly than ever in my life before that God might help me to keep my resolve.

February 3rd. My eyes were red with weeping so much. I went early to Alfred's room and begged him to go to Mother and make friends whilst I would be away at Sandal that day. I wished I might be at home but having promised Mrs. Henry, I must go. We arrived for dinner at 3 o'clock and Mrs. H. is well but must lie on the sofa a great deal lest she have another miscarriage. Young Paley (grandson of Archdeacon Paley[2]) joined us at dinner. I like Mrs. Henry much better now than I ever thought I could and yet still I am surprised, very much surprised, that Henry could have married her. She is exceptionally plain, very much marked with smallpox and wears her hair tied behind in long ringlets. After we had tea at 8 o'clock we played the piano and sang duets. Ann and I sat in our bedroom till after midnight, talking, and brushing and curling our hair. When I slept I had a frightening dream and woke Ann by my screaming.

February 4th. Mrs. H. had breakfast in bed and Henry urged us to stop till tomorrow; Ann agreed but I felt very uneasy and would have given anything to go home but they over-ruled me and Henry sent his clerk to ask Mother's permission and collect my music book if she said

I might stay – which she did. Mrs. Henry was not so well today but after dinner she played on the guitar and sang and Henry had no eyes or ears for anyone else. Ann and I sat up again brushing our hair and talking till after one o'clock.

February 5th. We arrived home at 1 o'clock and found Mother and Alfred quite well and friendly.

February 17th. My 23rd Birthday and I think I am now almost getting to be an old maid.

February 22nd. Mother and I went to Flanshaw. Grandmother was fairly well. We were talking about curing bacon and ham; some of ours was spoiled this year and grandmother said theirs was very good so we asked Ann (grandmother's maid) how she did it and she told us that the reason theirs was always good was because she always offered up a special prayer[3] before salting it. Poor Anna!

February 23rd. Sunday. Went to Chapel and Sunday school and Mrs. Holdsworth and I agreed to teach our girls to write. Mr. Crawford from Mill Hill Chapel in Leeds preached. I did not like the sermon. In the evening I sat a long time at my window watching the moon. It was very beautiful, until nearly 7 o'clock.

February 25th. My cousin Eliza Wood is 16 today. Mrs. D. and John called about more repairs they wish Mother to do for them. Cousin Ann lent me three of Beethoven's Waltzes which I intend to copy into my book. Ann and I had a long talk about the Sunday school scholars.

February 28th. Mother, Alfred and I went to drink tea with my Uncle Wood. Jane paid much attention to Alfred and he was in very good spirits. But I am sure the admiration is mostly on Jane's part. We were all very agreeable.

[1] Toothpicks were in demand and used generally and regularly at that time, but tooth brushes were not used until late Victorian days. Medical men used to assure people that the teeth and skin of healthy adults were self cleaning.

[2] William Paley died in 1805 and was a famous divine and writer on religious philosophy. His best known works were 'Evidence of Christianity' and 'Principles of Moral and Political Philosophy'. The first named was for many years regarded as a divinity text book at Cambridge.

[3] This prayer of Anna's seems to be a 'left over' from the days of witchcraft and incantations. But something was certainly needed at that time and maybe prayer was better than nothing. It indicated a willingness to do a good job. There were no Health Inspectors before 1842 – there were no food inspectors until a much later date and rinderpest was rampant in Europe. Robertson Scott records that in the first half of the 19th century about 4,000 cattle a week died of that disease in Britain. Diseased and maimed animals were often killed 'to save their lives'. Animals were quite generally slaughtered in the public streets near to the butcher's stalls – a district known as 'the shambles'. The flesh was displayed for sale on trestles or wooden blocks, exposed to flies, dust and dirty fingers. The butcher's blocks were often composed of cross sections of trees of gigantic girth – still bark-encrusted and very spectacular and very insanitary. There was very little over-wintering of stock except such animals as were required for breeding or Christmas fare. Every autumn a great slaughtering took place and the meat was cured for winter use. This salting-down was not done by experts but was the responsibility of the householder. As a result, much unhealthy meat was inexpertly cured and the results were reflected in skin troubles and digestive disorders. Eggs were cheap and plentiful, if the numbers reported to be used as missiles at public demonstrations gives a true estimate of the situation. Milk was fairly cheap and fairly dirty. Cream cost 5d to 6d a pint. There was no herd-testing in those days and Bovine T.B. was rampant. Handmilking was done under incredibly dirty conditions and the milkman made his rounds in a milk-float – a kind of low-slung dog-cart. Cans and dippers of assorted sizes were used and the milk poured from larger to smaller containers through a piece of muslin by way of filter. This muslin extracted flies, moths, hairs and other large foreign bodies and no doubt added innumerable invisible germs. Fortunately, it was generally considered that milk was not a drink for adults, except when boiled and well laced with rum. The high rate of infant mortality was due in some part to the fact that babies were fed warm but *not* boiled milk and there was no general knowledge of sterilisation of milk bottles or containers.

Chapter 14

Enter Victoria

THE journals covering the period between February 1834 to May 1837 are amongst the missing. When the story begins again many once-familiar names have gone. Mother is now always referred to as 'dearest Mother' and Clara's thoughts are centred more and more on her spiritual and temporal well being. The new book begins with this prayer – 'O God Almighty, bless to my use this record of my time, grant that I may make use of every means of improvement and so faithfully to write this journal that it may be a means of self examination and incite me to good so that I may in some degree prepare myself for Thy presence. Amen.'

May 2nd. I was very ill and did not rise till noon. Then dearest Mother and I called on Mrs. Shaw and on to Flanshaw to visit John. We walked back through the fields and gathered wood anemones. I wore my new bonnet – a new fashionable wide open shape which I think quite ugly. I cannot say I like it the least little bit.

May 5th. We had much company. Mr. Cannon came and sat by me on the sofa, but very soon I got up and walked away and was much provoked to find myself blushing. The subject chosen for this first meeting of our Literary Society was 'Is self love the governing principle of our nature?' I read an extract from a sermon of Stern's. Miss Heald read from The Spectator and Miss Holdsworth from Dr. Alexander's Phenological lecture – the part about 'self esteem' instead of 'self love'. Miss Hennell read a paper of her own composition and astonished us all completely. It was certainly well written – about stars and comets and earthquakes, volcanoes, moon, sun and the

Divine Essence – nothing whatever about 'self-love'. We were all quite puzzled and her explanation of its application only rendered it the more obscure. The others read various extracts from sermons and essays and encyclopedias and there followed a great deal of conversation and then we decided that self love was *not* the governing principle of our lives. We then served cake and wine which is contrary to the rules, but as it was the very first meeting everyone seemed pleased and enjoyed the occasion very much.

May 6th. Went to Uncle John's. Miss Ann Holdsworth was there and they were looking over our Chapel register. I found that Cousin Ann was born in April 1800. Later we walked through the fields to Stanley and gathered primroses and in the evening I lined my bonnet with white muslin and put velvet ribbon strings on it.

May 7th. Sunday. Mr. Cannon preached a continuation of last week's sermon. I received the sacrament. The service was rather different and most affecting and very beautiful and I prayed earnestly. We let the scholars out of Sunday school early to watch a military funeral, but Ann and I stayed in the Chapel to prepare the copy books. There is to be a meeting of Ministers at Bradford next Wednesday. Mr. Cannon is going and he wants us to accompany him.

May 8th. I am enjoying the study of French again with Annie O'Dwyer. Mr. Cannon called to ask dearest Mother if she and I would go to Bradford and after much persuasion she agreed, provided that the coach fare cost not more than 8/– each.

May 10th. Dearest Mother and I left home soon after nine. She travelled in a hackney coach with Mrs. Johnstone, and Mrs Marriott and I with Mr. Cannon, Misses Hennel, Alexander and Annie O'Dwyer in an open Barouche. It was very cold and at Morley we came into a violent storm. We were very merry about it and covered our heads with a mackintosh to keep off the snow. We got to Bradford at about 11.30 and after resting at the inn we went on to the Chapel at 12 o'clock. It is a very old place indeed and much smaller than ours in Wakefield, but they have a nice organ. The congregation consists of only about four families, with the exception of a few poor people. Mr. Turner of Halifax gave the prayers and Mr. Wickstead preached; the text was 'Lord, I believe, help thou mine unbelief'. It was a particularly beautiful sermon. It affected me to tears. The business of the Tract Society was transacted with Mr. Johnstone in the Chair and Mr. Wickstead read the report in a very nice way. He is so calm and self-possessed. He read the reports of the Tract Distributing Society of Leeds and York and Mr. Lupton of Leeds thanked them. When we got back to the inn at about 3 o'clock the gentlemen sent a deputation inviting the ladies to dine with them, which we agreed to do. When we came to the dining room Mr. Wickstead offered me his arm and I found myself seated between him and old Mr. H. and quite apart from dearest Mother and the others and at first I was a little concerned but Mr. Johnstone was quite close and Mr. Crawford, and they were all so kind that I soon felt quite at ease. I was careful not to take too much wine – there were so many toasts to be drunk. We drank to the health of the King and of Princess Victoria and then Mr. Turner and Mr. Wickstead and many more. We left for home at half past seven and it was a fine warm evening. I sat in the corner of the carriage and listened to the others talking over the occurrences of the day but I did not join in as my head ached and I was tired but I had enjoyed the day, just as they all had done, very much indeed.

May 13th. Dearest Mother and I called at Mrs. Cannon's and then went to look at the fashions at Mrs. Day's and dearest Mother ordered a black silk bonnet and then we called at my Uncle John's. Mary had had some leeches on her throat last night and was very poorly.

May 14th. Sunday. Saw John Clarkson and Mrs. John at Chapel. We gave the scholars a holiday as it was Whitsunday. In the evening the sermon was on the text 'give thanks unto God for all things through Jesus Christ' and I felt more devotional than I have felt recently.

May 15th. Called at Miss Heald's to ask her and Miss Hennel to drink tea with us on Thursday. I met Mr. Cassell as I came back. He had left Morley at 6 o'clock, breakfasted at Sandal and was going back to Morley for a Freemasons' dinner at four. I went on to my Uncle John's to ask them to come on Thursday also and my cousin John walked along to the library with me. Later, dearest Mother and I called at my cousin Henry's. Mrs. H. was lying on the sofa, she was punctiliously polite as usual. Little John is a lovely child and seems to have taken wonderfully to me (very unlike his papa!). At 8 o'clock Mr. and Mrs. Whitaker called.

May 16th. We walked to Lupset; a lovely morning. Miss Alexander is not well, in a cold, so cannot come on Thursday. We then called to tell Miss Watson to come to sew next week as poor Miss Dickenson is very ill and cannot sew now. I went to the meeting of our Literary Society at Miss Heald's. The subject was 'May'. As I was President it was my duty to write up the report. We finished at about 8 o'clock. Ann came along home with me and she seems to think Mary is in a poor way of health. She also told me that she had heard that poor Mrs. Benjamin has been taken to a Private Asylum; I hope this is not true.

May 18th. Much company today. I made tea in the room and Hannah handed it around. After tea we had music and sang duets and later danced several sets of quadrilles. Cousin John and his wife sang one of Moore's Melodies very well and Miss Heald sang several songs in Italian most beautifully. Caroline O'D. sang as ill as ever. Miss Hennel plays the piano brilliantly.

May 24th. The 21st birthday of the Princess Victoria.[1] The earl of Mexbro' came to lay the first stone of the new Corn Exchange and there were great rejoicings in the town and a large procession of Freemasons. We dined early and went to the library to watch the celebrations.

Northgate, from an engraving by T. Kilby in 1853.

May 26th. I took a musk plant and some flowers to Miss Heald. Mr. Cannon came in whilst I was there and we arranged to go together this evening. Mr. C. teased me and said he supposed we must leave there soon after 8 o'clock as I cannot be out later; they laugh at my coming home early but I think it rather unkind because they know dearest Mother objects to late hours and I feel it my duty to do as she wishes. However, we went to Miss Alexander's and then to Lupset Hall where we admired the gardens and the Picture Gallery, the coloured glass windows and fine black oak staircase. We walked back to Miss Alexander's for supper and there were crab sandwiches, amongst other good things. We stayed till after 10 o'clock and while walking home Miss Hennel told me about her sister's illness. She was in bed for two years and never spoke for six months. It was 11 o'clock when we got home very tired but dearest Mother was not at all vexed.

May 28th. Sunday. I dreamed last night that I watched my own funeral procession, then I realised that it is just 3 years today that my dear Alfred died – just thirteen days after his 21st birthday. It put me in low spirits for the rest of the day. I went to Chapel and Sunday school but came home early.

May 30th. Went to the library and got the letters of Lady M. W. Montague which are just published. Our Literary Society meeting is held today at Mrs. Holdsworth's and the subject is 'Home'. Most of the members dealt humorously with the subject and it was a most pleasant meeting but I felt ill, having a cold and a headache.

June 1st. Miss Marshall called and she and I took a walk to Pindar Fields. She told me that Mr. Wickstead is to marry Miss Jane Lupton. We called at my Uncle John's and found poor Mary very ill and scarcely able to speak. Mr. Robinson called and did nothing but extol the game of chess. Mr. Cannon and his brother William were there and William sang several songs very excellently. He told me how poorly he thought I looked. Mrs. Shepherd was most agreeable and when Hannah came for me at half-past nine I told her to wait. I stayed for supper and then (in spite of Mr. Cannon's persuasions) came away. It was then after 11 o'clock but dearest Mother was not at all angry with me.

June 3rd. We walked to Flanshaw and found John well but high in liquor. It was a beautiful day and our 'Chateau' as Miss Hennel calls it, looked very lovely. I often wish we lived there, but Mother cannot be persuaded to do so.

June 5th. Reading a book by Miss Stickney (or rather Mrs. Elles, for she was married this week). It is called 'Pretension' and is exposing the folly of people who educate their daughters to be governesses – often farmers' daughters who would be much better employed at home. It is a serious work and insists on the importance of a deep sense of religion. I dare say there is much in it to which Unitarians would not agree, but I often think that Unitarians do not think as much as they should of the thorough change of heart and that there is much truth in what our enemies say of us, that we set too much store on our own holiness and expect to win heaven by our virtues and that we are in fact cold. I must lend this book to Mr. Cannon.

June 11th. Sunday. Mr. Cannon preached from the words 'so teach us to number our days that we may apply our hearts unto wisdom'. It was occasioned by a dreadful accident which happened last week; a steam-packet going from Hull to Gainsbro' was blown up, owing to carelessness, before it left the pier and fifty people were killed in an instant. Mr. Cannon gave a beautiful sermon and it is such a pity he is to give up. There was a meeting after the service and Mr. Cannon read a letter from Mr. Higginson saying that he too had given up the ministry and was preparing to be an engineer so he cannot take Mr. Cannon's place.

June 13th. Went to Mrs. Day's about my new gown and we met Mr. and Mrs. Scatcherd and Mary and Fanny who are here for the breaking up of the Proprietary school. After dining we went with them to the school. A Mr. Keeling had been the examiner and he gave a very good report of their attainments. The head boy read his prize essay and many prizes and certificates of Honour were given. Watson and Samuel both had prizes. It was a very hot day and the room very crowded, we were glad to come home to drink tea.

June 14th. Mr. and Mrs. Whitaker called. Mrs. Whitaker is stouter than ever, really immense. I never saw a woman so stout. We went to Barrett's gardens but it began to shower so we came home and sang duets and played. Mr. Whitaker was quite astonished that I could play the accordion so well. He seemed well amused and they stayed till after 10 o'clock. Somehow I have not half the affection for Mrs. Whitaker[2] that I used to have.

June 17th. We walked in Barrett's garden with my Aunt Wood and Mary Ann and William. We each chose plants to the value of half our subscriptions. We got geraniums, petunias, calceolarias, a few pansy slips and a heath. My uncle John sent word that Mary was worse and they have sent to Leeds for Mr. H.

June 18th. Sunday. Mr. Cannon preached a very old sermon; I almost knew it word for word. There is a subscription being taken up to present a piece of silverplate to Mr. Cannon when he leaves.

June 19th. Mrs. Beaumont and old Mrs. Cannon came to drink tea. They are both very provoked about Mr. Cannon's leaving the Chapel. Later we went to drink tea at the Burton's. Mr. W. showed us a great quantity of beautiful engravings. It was a very pleasant evening.

June 23rd. Awoke depressed and thinking about dear Alfred. I try to persuade dearest Mother to sell Hardwick and pay off the mortgages but she is resolved not to do so. I wept bitterly and then felt better. In the evening cousin Ann and I walked to Stanley and by the fields to Hatfield Hall, it was a long walk but a lovely evening. Ann is quite convinced that Mary will never get better.

June 25th. Sunday. William Johnstone and his bride were at the Chapel. I am sure I wish them much happiness. Alfred was so fond of William who is just starting life with all its troubles ahead. How much happier is my dear Alfred with all his troubles ended! Mr. Cannon preached his farewell sermon. He ended by telling us that it was not without long and painful deliberation that he had determined to give up the Chapel; he said he felt compelled, as he had a sense of being deficient in some way and that he would not seek a new appointment. It was most affecting and many of us were in tears.

June 27th. Very hot day. Our next meeting is to be at Mrs. O's and I went this morning to the library to find something on our subject – 'decision of character', but found nothing, so went on to Flanshaw with Miss Tootall, Annie O. and Miss H. and borrowed chairs for them from the house and the two of them sat and sketched the old Hall, whilst Annie and I amused ourselves talking and walking in the fields until nearly 8 o'clock and we were weary and famished.

June 28th. Called at Miss Marshall's to see if there was anything in her encyclopedia about decision of character and again found nothing. Went to my Uncle John's. The Princess Victoria is proclaimed Queen[3] and the gentlemen of the town formed a procession and in Wood Street they were joined by the Cavalry and paraded the streets. We all went to my aunt Wood's and watched it all from her windows. The Literary Society meeting was well attended but we are to give up the meetings now until the last week in August.

[1] This day was in fact the 18th Birthday of the Princess, though Clara and many other people in England believed it to be her 21st. William IV had proclaimed that the day be a Public Holiday to celebrate the 'legal majority' of the Princess Victoria. There were processions, banquets, balls and other nation-wide festivities. William IV, who was in poor health, was determined that in the event of his death, the Duchess of Kent (whom he detested) should not be made Regent. He therefore made the Princess 'of age' by Royal Proclamation when she was only 18. He died just a month later and had he not taken this step when he did, England would have had another regency period.

[2] Stout Mrs Whitaker is 'dear Eb' of earlier years.

[3] There is no mention in the Journal of the death of King William IV on the 20th of June. This omission is entirely in keeping with the attitude, both then and since, to that monarch. He seems to have been a man of outstanding insignificance. We speak of Georgian, Regency, Victorian, Edwardian but who ever says 'Williamsian'? It is not just because it is a clumsy word; a generation which

Wood Street, with Music Saloon on right, from an engraving by T. Kilby in 1853.

can accept 'de-escalation' and 'containerisation' could well take 'Williamsian' in its stride. It is one of the just verdicts of time that William IV should be unsung, but nevertheless his short reign covered the most momentous seven consecutive years in the entire history of England.

This greatness was not due to the king but to those Ministers of the Crown who ruled the land through the reformed Parliament. In his 'Short History of the English Peoples', J. R. Green wrote: 'no ministry has ever wrought greater or more beneficial changes than the Whig Ministry of Lord Grey and Lord Melbourne'. Amongst the achievements of their ministries were Parliamentary Reform and the abolition of slavery – a Municipal Corporation Act was brought in and the monopoly of the East India Company and many other monopolies were abolished. For the first time the Government accepted some responsibility for education. New Poor Laws were formulated eradicating many of the worst features of the old order, and Civil Marriages and marriages of dissenters were legalised. Many vexatious taxes were abolished.

The Police Force, introduced by Peel in 1829 had been employed only in parts of the city of London. It was in the eighteen thirties that it was extended to serve provincial towns where it was sorely needed in the new overcrowded industrial areas. It was estimated that one person in every twenty-two was a criminal (as criminals were reckoned at that time). A famous Scottish judge commented that most of the other twenty-one might be 'nane the waur o'a hanging'. The Police Force was at first regarded as a form of tyranny and it took many years to reconcile people to the idea. Before Peelers came into the picture the only means of controlling mob violence was by calling out the Militia. There had been little protection from petty crime and the odds were usually on the transgressors.

The reform of the Poor laws was well overdue. Each Parish had previously been responsible for its own poor; there had been no government or public money available. A poor rate was struck in rural areas by the J.P.'s and in urban areas by the Poor Law Guardians of the Parish. The system had its advantages as it prevented the development of wandering bands of beggars, but it tended to create a permanent local pauper population – a sort of 'mini-caste' system which was demoralising for everyone concerned. It was calculated that one person in every eleven was a pauper and the poor relief was equated to wages not to cost of living. This suited the employer but was tragic for the worker. It was grossly unfair to classes other than industrialists and those who lived on their rent rolls. The industrialists paid miserably low wages and the gentry subsidised that wage bill by paying increasingly big poor rates. Abandoned children (and in those days there were many) usually became the responsibility of the Parish and remained so until they had completed their seven years of apprenticeship. However, it was a fact that most Parish orphans died in infancy and very few of them lived to the age of twelve or thirteen years. The system of apprenticeship was introduced in the reign of Elizabeth I and to its observance we probably owe the long record of excellence of British craftsmanship. It made sure that no man be a 'Jack of all trades and master of none'. Boys became apprenticed to a recognised 'master' at the age of thirteen or fourteen and were bound for seven years. The plan did not apply to girls who generally drifted into domestic service. C. M. Trevelyan, quoting from Clapham, wrote that those so employed 'were 50% more numerous than all the men, women, boys and girls in the cotton industry put together'. Cotton manufacturing was the biggest industry in Lancashire and the Midlands at that time.

The registration Act of 1836 legalised Civil marriages and marriages in non-conformist churches, providing that the Government Registrar be duly notified. Before that date only marriages in the Established Churches were strictly legal. This had been the case since 1753 when Lord Hardwicke's Marriage Bill had so enacted. It is true that Courts of Law accepted as evidence the entries in pedigrees, family bibles and Church or Chapel records but these were concessions and not rights. It would be rather interesting to know the percentage of technical 'bastards' in England between the years 1753 and 1836.

The Municipal Corporation Act of 1835 provided for the setting up of Town Councils chosen and elected by the people. Aldermen were, however, nominated by the elected Councillors and the Mayor was chosen from the ranks of the Aldermen. Thus matters of high consequence were still in the hands of the more élite which was no doubt just as well considering the lack of education of the majority of citizens before the introduction of free schooling in 1870.

These and many other reforms of Grey and Melbourne paved the way for the pomp and circumstance of the Victorian era and helped to establish in Britain a new respect for the Ten Commandments.

Chapter 15

Elections and Riots, Anti-Cruelty Society

JULY 2nd. Went to Chapel and Sunday school. Mr. Cannon administered the Sacrament for the last time; a most affecting service. I shall never like any other preacher so well and I know I owe him a great deal. Had it not been for him I would never have thought it my duty to receive the Sacrament, I thus would have lost a great means of religious improvement. A Mr. Roberts preached in the afternoon. It was so very hot that it was hard to be attentive in spite of ones best endeavours.

July 3rd. Went to look at the shops with Mary and Fanny. There was a large meeting of Mr. Gaskell's friends and supporters who met him and escorted him to the White Hart, where he addressed them. We stood a little time in the church yard, but R. the grocer, offered us a place in his window. He brought chairs and we had a very good view. Of course we heard nothing, but could see that he was very favourably received.

July 10th. Not feeling well and obliged to keep taking Camomile tea. We are thinking of going to Harrogate again in a few days time. There was a great storm of thunder and lightening just as we returned from walking in Barrett's gardens and all my old fears returned, though I try to reason with myself and to trust in God but I cannot overcome my fears.

July 15th. St Swithun's day[1] and much rain fell, to the consternation of poor Hannah. I went into town in the morning and bought books for prizes for my Sunday school scholars.

July 20th. Mr. and Mrs. Turner called to tell us that Sarah Ann died last week and was buried in the mausoleum yesterday. The family sent me a pair of white gloves.

July 24th. Dearest Mother and I walked to Flanshaw to see John and called at Adam's to order wine. There is great excitement now about the elections. Mr. Lascelles has come forward again and his supporters have tried every method of winning over Mr. Gaskell's adherents. Amongst other methods, they gave a 'tea-drinking' last Monday to some 4,000 women and there was all kinds of drunkenness attendant on it. It is acknowledged that victory is very uncertain and both parties are trembling about results. I intend to keep as much aloof as possible. Mr. Lascelles has been presented today with a splendid blue flag by the ladies of the Tory Party.

July 25th. Today is Nomination day. We went down Wood street at 10 o'clock and met the Misses Burrels and so went with them to the hustings. The Parties seemed to be equally divided and excitement very great indeed – no one without a blue or yellow ribbon. The Blues had got placards announcing the election of Tories for Hull and the Yellows insisted upon having them taken away, which, after some dispute, was done. The Yellows seemed very violent. Janet Burrel seemed quite frightened of a riot and squeezed my arm so much that it bruised. Annie O'Dwyer arrived with the Gaskells, Dr. Naylor proposed and Mr. Leatham seconded him. Mr. Barff proposed Mr. Lascelles and Mr. Black seconded him. We left the hustings before the speeches ended but were told that things went in Mr. Gaskell's favour.

July 26th. Feeling very poorly and lay in bed till noon. Mr. Cannon called and said he had been told that there was not the least chance for Mr. Gaskell. A large party who had promised him their votes had disappeared this morning. At 4 o'clock my Aunt Wood called and told us that Mr. Lascelles was elected by a majority of 26 votes. Cousin Ann came in a little later protesting about 'the triumph of iniquity'. The Yellows are dreadfully disappointed and furious; feeling never ran so high in Wakefield before this.

July 28th. Walked with dearest Mother in Barrett's gardens and on returning found old Mrs. Cannon and Mr. Cannon at our house. We gathered black currants and cherries for them. Am reading 'Vivian Grey'.

July 30th. Sunday. Mr. Cannon preached today, as he had promised he would. It was a most moving sermon. I sat with my class and prayed more fervently than I have done for a long time. At Sunday school we taught the scholars to write and to do accounts. I have three new girls who cannot read at all. They give me much trouble but I feel I must help the very slow ones. There is talk everywhere of the instances of bribery at the recent elections. I felt so very low spirited that I wept bitterly in my bedroom. It is a long time since I experienced such depression of spirit and I could not account for it.

July 31st. Nomination day for the County elections held in Wakefield. The three candidates are Morpeth, Strickland and Worsley. Vehicles of all descriptions began to arrive very early in the morning with colours and music. Mr. Scatcherd came and left his pocket book and fifty-five pounds with Mother for safety before going into town. We went into town just after 11 o'clock to get a cake at Glover's and bought ribbon at Binn's. There were so many people around and we could scarcely proceed. They say that there were 40,000 assembled in town and it was all confusion and many shops were closed so we were glad to get home by back ways and side lanes. A little before 2 o'clock Mr. Scatcherd came back in a great fright to tell us that there was a riot in town. It began when the Yellows from Huddersfield came up with the Blues and tried to drive them off their ground. They had quite evidently come for that purpose as they were armed with sticks and bludgeons. Mr. Scatcherd was in the Woodman Inn, which is a Blue House and when the riot began he escaped with difficulty, for brickbats and stones were flying in all directions and many people were knocked down and trampled upon. He waited a short time with us and then went back to get more news. Some people who had been fighting came and begged for water and they said the fray was continuing as fierce as ever. Mr. Scatcherd returned and told us that the Riot Act had been read and that the military had been sent for from Leeds. He went back to Morley after drinking tea very early as he feared they might have heard news in Morley and would be uneasy about him. The soldiers arrived at about 5 o'clock but by then the mob in town had dispersed but there were several skirmishes on Westgate Common. Mrs. Hind and her daughter called later. They had seen much of the riot and she says she never saw anything so dreadful and she saw many people seriously injured. They say it was all the wicked Whigs and that Mr. Craven was to be blamed and that it was he who gave the signal for the riot to start. Others say it was all Mr. Castle's fault and that the whole thing was a Tory Radical[2] trick.

August 1st. My aunt Wood and William called and they told us that poor Mr. Carter of Ossett was dead after being dreadfully injured in the affray yesterday. He was only twenty-seven and his poor wife is expecting a baby. They sent for her, but he was dead when she arrived. We went with my aunt along Wood Street and what a sight it was! Not a pane of glass and in the Woodman Inn many of the window frames had been torn out and copingstones had been pulled from the wall to be used as brickbats. The iron gate and railing of the Court House were broken off and the windows broken. It was a desolate place and groups of people were gathered together talking it all over.

August 2nd. Mr. Scatcherd called to get his pocket book and his money. He had come to bring the boys back to school and he invited us to go to Morley next week to stay for a few days.

August 3rd. Cousin Ann came to tell us the state of the poll which she says is very unsatisfactory. We picked red currants for wine today. Mr. Cannon came and brought Mr. Cameron to introduce him to us. He has an awkward

Kirkgate, below the Church steps, from an engraving by T. Kilby in 1853.

manner and has immense feet and huge white hands and a black shock of hair, a really handsome forehead and a very Scottish accent. We talked of course, about the riots and then about poetry and I began to think that he is really a clever man, even a genius, but alas! *not* a gentleman. They say he is only twenty-nine, but he looks forty and he writes poetry.

August 6th. Sunday. Chapel and Sunday school and I prepared my scholars for doing their work without me next week when I shall be away. They are good and I know they will conduct themselves just as if I were there. I set copies for them and left everything in order. I drank tea at my uncle John's. Mr. Whitaker was there and said how delighted he was with Mr. Roberts. In the evening Mr. Cameron's text was 'be ye perfect as your Father who is in Heaven is perfect'. I cannot give any account of his sermon but I know I heard something more beautiful than I have ever heard before, so poetical and exquisite that one forgets his odd accent. I did not admire his prayers as much as the sermon, they are not as devotional as I think they should be, but we are all quite delighted with his preaching.

August 7th. Spent the evening at Flanshaw. It was quite delightful but rather cold. I wish I may not fall in love with Mr. Cameron. I fear I have thought much about him today, more than I can understand or approve. However, we go away to Morley and then to Harrogate and I am glad of that.

August 8th. Annie O'Dwyer told me that she met Mr. Cameron at a large evening party last night and everybody was charmed by him. I am glad to hear this as it tempers some of the romance with which I had invested him and if he likes these large parties he will fall in my opinion too. Dearest Mother and I called at my Aunt Wood's and Mary Ann and I had a long talk about getting married. I am sure I do not know what is the matter with me, I have been very unsettled lately and not had the same joy in religious duties as I used to have. I am growing worldly and discontented and selfish and the dread of death grows upon me. O God, change my heart and receive me into Thy favour. Amen.

August 9th. James came for us with the carriage at 11 o'clock and we had a pleasant drive to Morley. Only Mary, Fanny and young Oliver are at home now and Oliver is a fine child and very like Fanny, so good tempered. After dinner Mrs. Wordsworth arrived with the two Miss Hursts. Miss Hurst told us that the 'Rev.' Thomas Clarkson is losing his congregation very fast – and I am not surprised.

August 12th. Mr. and Mrs. Scatcherd, dearest Mother and I went to Leeds. We went to the glovemakers and bought several pairs and I bought some shoes and in the Central Market I bought a book of Burn's poems for 1/3d. We were home by 5 o'clock and I had a very bad headache. John H. came to drink tea. He is down from Cambridge where he has been for some time but is just as clownish and backward as ever.

August 13th. Went to Church and Mr. Cassel preached about preaching the gospel to the heathen. A very poor sermon but it lasted only ten minutes. In the afternoon I went with Mary and Fanny to see their Sunday school. It is a big room but they have not as many scholars as we have. In the evening Mr. S. read us part of a beautiful sermon that Mr. Cannon had lent him.

August 16th. The Swindens have had a pretty little greenhouse built, leading off from their drawing room and we spent much time looking at the plants. Sarah Swinden and I played several pieces, but as Mr. Scatcherd never asks Sarah to play when she visits them Mr. Swinden did not ask Mary to play and I know Mr. Scatcherd was provoked. Several callers came whilst we were there and Mrs. Swinden introduced me as 'Her Majesty' for so many people say I have a great likeness to our Queen. We played cards and I was very weary and wished myself at home.

August 18th. We set off for home at half past nine. Mrs. Scatcherd and Mary with us, to spend a few days in Wakefield. When we had gone little more than a mile, James remembered that he had left a letter of Mr. Scatcherd's behind so we sat in the carriage whilst he sent a boy back to the house to fetch it and so we did not arrive home till after 11 o'clock. Then we went into town to the corset makers. Mary S. leans very much to one side and they fear that she may grow up deformed and hope that a corset might correct that. I think perhaps it is already too late. Watson and Samuel dined with us and later we played cards and Mary refused to drink tea and insisted on having beer. She is a very spoiled child now.

August 19th. Mr. Cannon and old Mrs. Cannon called and he left her with us whilst he went on to Lupset. Miss Burrel also called. They are collecting subscriptions for a piece of silverplate to give Mr. Daniel Gaskell and dearest Mother gave them 5/–.

August 21st. Feeling very poorly today and am drinking camomile tea. Jane and I went walking and near the Cliff Tree Jane found a gold wedding ring with the words 'hope and love' written on the inside. I told her it must be a good omen for her. We called at the library on our way home hoping to find something about 'determination of character' for our next meeting and found Caroline O'Dwyer and Fanny Marshall there on a similar errand; but we found nothing so when I got home I sat down and wrote some wretched stuff. Later Miss Marshall and her brother called and they sang several duets together just as my darling Alfred and I used to do.

August 27th. Sunday. Mr. Cannon preached a very old doctrinal sermon and when the service was over those of the congregation who had attained the age of 21 stayed, and the clerk brought round to each person, two papers; one with Mr. Cameron's name and one with Mr. Roberts' and we each put into the box the one with the name of the preferred candidate. Dearest Mother and I both voted for Mr. Cameron though we were grieved to vote against Mr. Roberts. There were 62 for Mr. Cameron and only 8 for Mr. Roberts. As I went to Sunday school in the afternoon I met Mr. Cannon walking with Mr. Cameron and he said 'Well Miss Clarkson, here is your parson', and of course I said how very pleased I was.

August 30th. Mr. Cameron came to our Society meeting at my uncle John's and at Mr. Cannon's request he repeated some lines of Keats' 'Ode to a Nightingale' and then gave a criticism of it which I liked much better than the poem itself. He is going to give some lectures on poetry of which he seems very fond. Hannah came for me at 8 o'clock and Mr. Cannon took Ellen Tootal home and Mr. Cameron took Annie O'Dwyer – and that pleased nobody.

September 2nd. Called at my Aunt Wood's who seemed troubled about their affairs since the death of my uncle. The girls were lamenting about their dowries not being arranged so that they may get married. Mary Ann and I walked to Lowe Hill and Dirtcar – the same walk I used frequently to take with Mrs. Whitaker when she was still Miss Burton and I have not been there since she married.

September 3rd. Mr. Cameron preached a most learned and obscure sermon on the text 'God is truth'. Mr. Cannon sat in our pew with dearest Mother and then Mr. Cameron administered the Sacrament and delivered a most affecting address, but it was the very first time he had ever officiated and he had to go twice to ask Mr. Cannon how to proceed which I found most discomposing and I fear I derived no benefit. Then cousin Ann insisted on our returning with her to dine with them.

September 6th. Went with Jane and Fanny M. to the 'Society' meeting at Tootal's at Lupset. There we found the Holdsworths and O'Dwyers, cousin Ann and the rest of them. Ellen began to read some of Wordsworth and right in the midst of it Mr. Cameron and Mr. Cannon walked in. So Mr. Cameron read the poetry and in his great ecstasy he at last went down on his knees on the floor and held the book high to the candles which looked a little comical. We all walked home together and cousin Ann kept talking about animals as usual. She told Mr. Cameron that she always thought there was something about little pigs which greatly resembled human infants. I am now quite disenchanted by Mr. Cameron.

September 10th. Mr. Cameron preached a wonderful sermon which impressed me greatly. He came into the Sunday school later to talk with us. It is very sad about a member of our congregation – young Burkenshaw, a grocer; he stabbed a man whilst in a fit of passion and was taken to York Castle, as the man he stabbed is not expected to recover. Poor Burkenshaw was, I presume, overwhelmed by remose for his action and hanged himself in the Castle cell. Mr. Cameron had been to visit his mother and sister and he says their distress is pitiable.

September 11th. Jane and I walked along Pindar fields and passed the Pauper Asylum[3]. Coming home we were caught in a thunder shower.

September 13th. I went with Cousin Eliza and Emma to the Horticultural Meeting held in the Music Salon. It was very crowded. The fruits and the dahlias were very good, but it is no pleasure to me to see lovely flowers cut off the plants and stuck into little bottles. There were dishes of pansies and African marigolds and some quite beautiful house plants. The room was full of a very genteel company. Watson Scatcherd was at our house when we returned, reading 'Midshipman Easy'. The members of our 'Society' arrived at about 6 o'clock and Mr. Cameron came too.

September 14th. Jane and I went walking through Pindar fields and past the Pauper Asylum. When we came home cousin Ann came and Fanny Marshall and the Miss Scholls and Ann talked of her fondness for animals. We all argued with her and she became so provoked I thought she might weep. But we enjoyed it immensely and laughed a great deal, for we all think Ann is so foolish about animals.[4]

[1] St Swithun was Bishop of Winchester. When he died in 862 he was buried, as he had desired, in the church yard so that the 'sweet rain of heaven' might fall upon his grave. After his canonisation, the monks thought to honour him by removing his body to the Choir and July 15th was the day appointed for the transfer. However, it rained and continued to do so for forty days, so the monks realised that the saint preferred the graveyard and gave

up their idea of re-burial. This is the origin of the legend of St. Swithun's day which is a legend peculiar to England. However, many lands have a rain saint; in Scotland it is St. Martin, in Flanders St. Godeleive, and in France St. Médan.

[2] The Radicals took a sympathetic view of the Chartist Movement and in 1837 formulated the 'Peoples Charter'. Its chief aims were universal franchise, a secret ballot and payment for members of Parliament so that men other than those of the wealthy classes might represent the people at Westminster.

[3] The Pauper Asylum in Wakefield, built in 1817, was one of the first of its kind in the country. There had long been Private Asylums for those whose families could afford to pay, but for the poor there was no proper provision. The insane were restrained in work houses or the Common Prisons. They were often put into straight-jackets – quite frequently manacled or held in chains. The other inmates robbed them of their miserable food rations and they were usually treated with great brutality. The ill treatment of the violently insance was the result of an early belief that such creatures were possessed of devils. If prayers and holy waters failed, perhaps violence and torture might succeed.

The feeble minded were not usually unkindly treated, in fact, the gentle idiot was often regarded as a creature blessed of God and the Village Idiot was a privileged being. The Pauper Asylum in Wakefield was started in a very small way and eventually developed into a large and comprehensive Mental Hospital.

[4] It was at about this time that Ann had got a committee together to found an Anti-Cruelty Society. The S.P.C.A. had been founded in London in 1824 but it was not till the early years of Victoria's reign that it became a 'Royal' society and was put on a national footing. In 1837 it was found that two small organisations were already functioning in the Provinces – one in Liverpool and this one in Wakefield. These local societies eventually became absorbed by the National Society. When Ann Clarkson died, a monument was put up to her memory because of her work for animal welfare. It was situated in the middle of the street at the top of Westgate and consisted of a drinking fountain with chained iron drinking cup, a long horse trough and one below for dogs. What had been an amenity in the 19th century became a motorist hazard in the 20th. When last I saw it (in 1951) it had been drawn to the side of the road where it looked lost and forlorn and of no use to man or beast.

Chapter 16

Harrogate — Bone Houses

SEPTEMBER 16th. Mrs. Scatcherd came to Wakefield to take Watson and Samuel home and invited me to go back with them for a few days, but I refused as I knew dearest Mother would not wish me to go but I was very disappointed.

September 17th. Sunday. After the service this morning cousin Henry came to tell us that he had got a little daughter on Friday morning. Mr. Cameron stopped in the midst of his sermon to rebuke someone who was behaving ill; coming out of the Chapel I met Mr. and Mrs. Whitaker who offered to see me home, but I told them that Hannah always met me and that I never went out otherwise.

September 18th. Dearest Mother and I went to a lecture by Mr. Cameron on 'Sensation and the relation of man to external objects'. I liked it very well but fear I did not understand the whole of it. He must indeed be a very clever, devout and excellent man.

September 23rd. Hannah is very ill. We think perhaps it is the Cholera. We did everything we could for her and had to do much for ourselves.

September 24th. Sunday. Mr. Cameron's sermon quite electrified us all. He divided religions into three classes and then proceeded to point out the reasons which hindered doctrinal agreement; the Arminians, the Calvanists and the Unitarians. He said the Arminians or Church People hindered agreement by their formality. The 'Christian Fashionables' he called them, who parade with gilt edged prayer books, bowing and curtseying to each other and decorously repeating responses. The Calvanists, he said, prevented agreement by their bigotry and intolerance and he accused us Unitarians of indifference and apathy; in fact, he was most severe on us, accusing us of coldness and deadness and want of devotional feelings. My heart beat so that it was painful and I came home and was unable to eat. In the evening Mr. Cameron preached on the text 'the raindrops return not to heaven' and he went on to say that every human being lives for ever, in that his slightest word or action has an influence on others and they are felt from generation to generation. It is an awful thought and should be everpresent with us. We were all delighted by his eloquence and I felt quite ill with excitement and could not eat or sleep. Hannah is a little better, it is not the Cholera but she is still in bed.

September 25th. Dearest Mother, Eliza and I went to Mr. Cameron's second lecture. It was all rather obscure. He says there is no such thing as sound, taste, smell or colour without a sentient being; it all rests on our perception of them. I cannot really understand it all.

September 30th. Walked with Mr. and Mrs. S. to Sandal Castle Hill. A lovely morning. In the afternoon Mrs. S. and dearest Mother went into town but I lay on the sofa, feeling dizziness in my head which I think is caused by too much talking. Next week I intend to go out of mourning and must get some new coloured gowns before we go to Harrogate.

October 1st. Mr. Cameron stopped again in his sermon this morning to rebuke some people who were behaving ill. He said that the next time he sees any irreverent behaviour he will call on the offenders by name. The sermon lasted an hour and twenty minutes and we were all tired. He is really a Unitarian-Methodist and his actions are like those of a Methodist preacher.

October 2nd. Mrs. S. returned to Morley and dearest Mother and I went to Mr. Cameron's third lecture. He has had a platform erected in front of the pulpit and he lectured on the utility of metaphysical speculation and the subjective and objective worlds – just a little obscure, like last week's lecture.

October 4th. Dearest Mother and I walked to Sandal to call on Mrs. Henry Clarkson who had just come down stairs after her confinement. She looked very well and so did the dear little baby girl. I could not help thinking how different it all might have been, and for the rest of the day I was haunted by old memories of my feelings in those past years.

October 11th. Mr. Cannon went with us in the coach to Leeds and there left us. At the 'Rose and Crown', Mrs. Scatcherd joined us and we took the stage coach to Harrogate. Mr. Cannon told us that he begins to think Mr. Cameron too dogmatic. We arrived at our lodgings a little before 5 o'clock. Mrs. Benns has only ten other visitors now, several of them are people we have met on previous visits. There is a Mr. Crowther and a young man who plays on the clarinet and Mrs. S. and her daughter from London and an odd looking gentleman called 'Basket' who seems very nice and Mr. and Mrs. Hogg who were here before.

October 12th. We went to the wells and took the waters before breakfast and spent most of the day looking at the shops. Mrs. S. bought a cloak. After dinner someone mentioned the Luptons of Leeds and Mr. Hogg said what nice people they were, but added 'it is so sad that they are Jocinians'. Someone asked him if they were worse in any way on that account and he rushed from the room and returned with his Bible and began to read from the Epistle to the Hebrews and went on to say that his own salvation is secured through the death and sacrifice of Christ and that most of us live in a state of wilful blindness and that 'he that believeth not shall be damned'. It was a most distasteful performance which I trust will not be repeated.

October 13th. We drove to High Harrogate in a donkey carriage. I should say dearest Mother and Mrs. S. drove, but I walked as I disliked to distress the poor donkey which I feared was overloaded.

October 14th. We took the waters as usual before breakfast but I begin to fear they do not agree with me. We went in a donkey carriage to call on Mrs. H. and again I walked. In the evening some of us sat in the little drawing room in the moonlight and Mr. Cavell played on the flute. He is a very good looking young man, tall, fair, stoutish and very good tempered. This morning dearest Mother bought a beautiful length of French silk for me. Mrs. Hogg talked to me today about her life in Portugal. She was there when they had a great earthquake. She told me that the Catholics in Portugal were most intolerant and regarded her and her husband as heretics, without hope of Heaven. I agreed that such intolerance is regretable but she does not seem to realise that intolerance is one of her husband's chief characteristics.

October 15th. Sunday. We went this morning to the Harrogate Parish Church to hear Mr. Kenneon preach and I stayed indoors in the afternoon and read the Bible and talked to Miss S. from London who told me she used to live in Ireland and that she had run away from a boarding school there. In the evening I went with Mr. Cavell to the Calvanist Chapel.

October 16th. We breakfasted early and then set out for Studley Royal. Dearest Mother and I and Mrs. Scatcherd and Mrs. S. and her daughter in the carriage and the gentlemen accompanied us on horseback. It was a clear frosty morning and I never saw Fountains Abbey look so lovely. Mr. Cavell and I had long chats together. His father is a woollen manufacturer in Bradford and they have a warehouse and office in London. They are Methodists. Two of his sisters and his mother died in consumption. He has only one sister now who is seventeen and he is very devoted to her. He says Mr. Hogg has warned him to give up singing as it leads young men into sinful and evil company (meaning Jocinians I have no doubt). On the way home we stopped at Ripon and visited the Minister and the Bone House there.[1]

October 18th. Mr. and Mrs. Hogg departed today much to my content. Mr. Cavell sang and I played his accompaniments and helped him to copy some music. Mr. Basket is a most agreeable person. Miss S. told me today that someone had said to them that dearest Mother never permitted me to visit anywhere without her. I was most provoked and I know it could not have been anyone but Mrs. Scatcherd who said that to them.

October 21st. Mr. Cavell has a very bad cold. I helped him to copy music in the morning and he asked me where we lived in Wakefield. I gave him our address and he asked if he might call. I am sure I hope he will do so. We left for home in an open carriage and everyone was there to see us off.

October 26th. I wonder if Mr. Cavell will call. I wish he may today. Went into town and bought a quire of paper to make six copy books for my Sunday school scholars. At my Aunt Wood's we talked of Harrogate and had a long discussion about Unitarianism to which Mary Ann seems to have some leaning, owing (I believe) to the fact that Mr. S. is one.

October 29th. Sunday. Mr. Cameron preached again on the Christian Churches. It was rather abstruse; he spoke much of languages and seemed to forsee that the whole world would in the end speak just one language – the English. In the evening Mr. Cameron had proposed to give Dr. Channing's sermon on the evils of Calvinism but it was nearly 8 o'clock before he began to read, the rest of the time being taken up with his own remarks and views against Calvinism which were very severe. He says he has lived amongst them all his early life and that he knows that where Calvinism prevails there is also infidelity and scepticism.

October 30th. Copied music lent me by Mary Ann 'The light of other days' – one of Mr. C.'s favourite songs. Dearest Mother said she wished our Literary Society meetings would be given up and I answered crossly and unbecomingly. – Oh Lord, forgive me for it and grant that she may have forgiven me and forgotten it too. Amen.

November 1st. Mr. Cannon and Miss Heald called for me with a coach and then we called for Caroline and cousin Ann and drove to Miss Alexander's. She is always so very formal. We had our meeting in her dining room which is newly decorated in crimson and very handsome. We decided that in future, every third meeting should consist of poetry readings and we also agreed that Mr. Cameron be invited to join us at these meetings. We sat like a parcel of school girls and read in turns from the 4th canto of Childe Harold and so went on till 9 o'clock. Several of us were yawning for an hour and we were glad when the coach came for us.

November 2nd. Mary Ann and Eliza and cousin Ann came to drink tea. They talked about politics and then told ghost stories till they really frightened each other. I told them of my Harrogate adventures – some of them at least.

November 5th. Sunday. Dearest Mother said that as we were having guests for dinner we had better not stay to take the sacrament, but I could not agree to that and said I would dine at my uncle John's instead. Mr. Cameron preached on the Millennium and his address at the Sacrament service was most affecting. Mr. Cannon told us later that he objects very much to the way Mr. Cameron insists on leaving all the doors and windows open at the Chapel.

November 7th. Dearest Mother and I went to Mr. Lumb's office about sending notice to quit to John Dawson and Mr. Lumb said it should really have been sent before August 2nd. However, it will be sent and I hope John will agree, but I fear we shall have much trouble and anxiety about it. I begin to think that Mr. Cavell will not call on us now. I am sure it is all because of that nasty Mr. Hogg and his talk against Unitarians. I am sorry and I know he meant to when he asked for our address and asked if he might call.

November 9th. Walked with Mary Ann to Snow Hill Bar and on to Silcoates and then we walked in Barrett's gardens.

Today, a woman, a Mrs. Graham, ascended from Wakefield in a balloon. We saw it well from our gardens as it passed over East Moor and then it became enveloped in cloud and we saw it no more. Mr. and Mrs. Whitaker came to drink tea and they both seemed to be in low spirits. He played the accordion and I the piano. We sang 'Come dwell with me' which they seemed to like very well. I fear they are not truly happy. When they left I read part of my journal for 1832 and it made me see the vanity of all earthly things.

November 12th. Sunday. Mr. Cameron had to call out to the boys of the Sunday school who were sitting in the gallery, telling them to behave themselves. It was so windy last night and one of our windows was blown in.

November 13th. Fair Day. I fear that I have a bad cold and dare not go out, so read and studied French. Mrs. S. called. She told me she had seen Mr. Cavell in Harrogate after we left and that he was quite poorly, which did not surprise me; he was ill the day we left.

November 14th. Our 'Society' met at Mrs. O'Dwyer's. They were all there except Miss Alexander and the subject was 'the advantages of science and the education of the people'. It was all very dull and tedious and my head ached and it did not end until half-past nine.

November 20th. Feeling a little better after two weeks of feverish cold and a cough which is still quite troublesome. Cousin Ann came to sit with me and told me that Mr. Cameron had told them last night he wore no shoes or stockings until he was 12 years old – that was in Scotland. Miss Marshall came to drink tea, but she had brought her music and sang several songs; she practices her music for two hours every day.

November 23rd. My cousin Ann told me that Mrs. Henry is very ill indeed and they fear she has a consumption.

November 26th. Sunday. I was not well enough to go to Chapel so dearest Mother went alone. She was very delighted by Mr. Cameron's sermon. After the service there was a meeting about ventilating the Chapel. It seems that heat makes Mr. Cameron feel poorly. My dear Mother gave me a mixture of yeast and Port wine for my throat and I think it did me some good.

November 27th. Feeling much better and I am sure it is partly because of the Port and yeast. Mrs. Burton called and she told me that the Whitakers are looking for new lodgings. Mr. Whitaker's two boys have run away from school and come home, so they need a larger place. They have looked at a house in the lane and I sincerely hope they will not come so near. Henry Burton is making an assignment[2] and William does nothing but drink and is most quarrelsome.

December 3rd. Sunday. Set out to go to take Sunday school but met some of the children coming to tell me that they had a holiday as Mr. Cameron is having a respirator put on the roof because he dislikes the heat so the gallery could not be in use today. We went to Chapel and Mr. Cameron continued the sermon on Education. Ann sat in our pew and the gallery people all sat down stairs. Mr. Cameron rebuked us for the frivolity of our lives and spoke against pride – pride of birth and pride of wealth. I liked the sermon very well but some of them did not.

December 12th. Mr. James Day called and asked to see a diary that my dear Alfred kept of the work they did at the office. I did not go in to meet him and dearest Mother knew nothing of the matter, but I had treasured it and did not feel inclined to let anyone see it and particularly not this Mr. James Day. But I agreed to let dearest Mother show it to him and later I cried passionately as it brought back all my saddest memories.

December 17th. Sunday. Went to Chapel and Sunday school. I have a new scholar, a young Jewess whom Mr. Cannon had sent along. Her father is a Polish refugee. Cousin Ann told me that Mrs. Henry is very much worse. Mr. Cannon preached as Mr. Cameron is away in Bolton or London, we are not sure which. He read a sermon of Dr. Channings and we all thought it very dull after being used now to Mr. Cameron. We did not go to afternoon

Chapel as it rained too heavily and the roads were muddy and impassible.

December 18th. Went shopping with dearest Mother and bought materials and a bonnet and one of the new fashioned round combs for my hair which they are all wearing now. Later, we went to Sandal to visit Mrs. Henry. Cousin Henry seemed to be very low-spirited indeed about her. She had just been having leeches on and so was very ill. We sat a little while with Henry in the nursery. The wet nurse was there. The little boy is ill but the baby girl seemed well enough. We left quite soon and as we walked home it began to rain and it rained for the rest of the day and was very windy.

December 19th. A very wet day and I felt depressed and poorly. Annie O'Dwyer came in spite of the rain.

December 20th. There was a terrible storm in the night and so much rain that the flood waters reached to the Ship Inn in Kirkgate and 4,000 pounds worth of damage was done they say. At Horbury three large boats were seen on the highroad and there they still remain blocking the way. Three lives were lost at Bradford where a waggon load of timber was seen floating down the street like a ship at sea. There has not been such a flood for 30 years.

December 21st. I proposed to my cousins today that we start a Musical Society and they agreed joyfully. The subject for our next Literary Society meeting is to be 'who is the most perfect character in scripture next to our Saviour?' I thought of John the Baptist but I fear I cannot write anything good enough.

December 22nd. Dearest Mother sent a note to John Dawson asking him when he could allow Mr. Maud to look over the house, so he called later and was most polite but he does not want to go and says he is sure the place would not suit the Mauds. We went to call on my Aunt Wood and my cousins are eager to join this Musical Society and they are going to invite Eliza Marshall and Julia Harrison. We went then to call on Margaret Johnstone who has just returned from Burlington. Captain Johnstone came in whilst we were there and talked great nonsense as usual, but Eliza says he waltzes wonderfully well. On the way home we called at my Uncle John's and Henry was there. When Alverthorpe Hall was mentioned Henry said why not let it to him? Indeed! I pretended not to have heard him and did not reply.

December 23rd. We walked to Alverthorpe and saw John Dawson and then on to Flanshaw to see John and took him a spice-cake. We met one of dear dear Grandmother's pensioners and gave her 1/-, then called at Adam's and ordered a bottle of Port to be sent to her for Christmas. I wish I could help all the poor people I see everywhere. Christmas is such a general time for rejoicing but it brings back memories of the loved and lost ones who used to share these rejoicings with us.

December 24th. Sunday. Chapel, but it was dark so very early and we did not have afternoon Sunday school. Mr. Cannon preached as Mr. Cameron is still away.

December 25th. We dined at my Aunt Wood's. They had been at Sandal to church and Henry Dawson had preached and my aunt said that he 'sent all Jocinians to Hell' but that it was a very good sermon! We spent a very dull day with them.

December 26th. Dearest Mother went with Mr. Maud to look over the Hall. It is sadly in need of renovation. The Mauds fear that Hatfield Hall (where they live now) may be in some danger of subsidence from coal workings below just as Flanshaw is. That is why they want to come to Alverthorpe, but it may be too small for them. I prepared my essay for our meeting tomorrow.

December 27th. All our members came to the meeting at Miss Alexander's. Most of them read essays of their own composition. Cousin Ann had chosen Joseph as her subject and Caroline O'Dwyer had fixed on Job of all people; Ellen Tootal on Ruth. It was quite one of the most amusing meetings we have had, but I was ashamed of my own poor effort. Caroline is really one of the most irreverent girls I have ever met. She says she has never read the

Wakefield Market Place, from an engraving by T. Kilby in 1853.

Old Testament since she was six years old. She says it is no use at all and is all about a set of 'wicked old fellows'. She says someone told her to read the 1st Chapter of St. John as a proof of the trinity and she did, and was quite 'shocked'. Dearest Mother sent a coach for us at 9 o'clock and we were very merry as we drove back home.

December 29th. Drank tea at my Aunt Wood's and we settled the rules and agreed to call our new Society 'The Philharmonic' and arranged the first concert which is to be next week. Everyone is to perform four pieces of some kind – all of them sing except Emma and myself. Julia has a very deep voice but a very good one. Everyone is most joyful about the plans.

December 31st. Spent a restless feverish night and dearest Mother went alone to Chapel and came home delighted with a Mr. Giles of Liverpool who had preached, as Mr. Cameron is still away. I went with her in the afternoon as I felt a little better. Mr. Giles is a hunchback, a very tiny man with a beautiful voice. His prayer about the close of the year was most affecting. Mr. Cameron is going preaching all the country over.

[1] Bone Houses or Charnel Houses were quite numerous until very recent times. They were generally situated in ancient Cathedral towns or adjacent to the sites of ancient battles. In medieval times the church yard cemeteries were over-used and in making new graves old ones were disturbed. The unearthed bones were reverently deposited in church crypts or other sacred precincts. Chantries were frequently built to house the bones collected on the field after a great battle so that Masses and prayers might be offered for the fallen. In the course of time the Bone Houses lost their respected status and became show places. In the volume on Kent in 'The King's England', Arthur Mee states that the Bone House at Hythe is the sole remaining one in England today. He says that 'within the very walls of this old church are dead men's bones piled up in rows, with something like 1,000 skulls all looking down'. Some of the skulls are said to date from the time of Roman occupation and one has evidently undergone the operation of trepanning. The incision must have been done with a flint instrument and that the patient lived many years after the operation is proved by the state of the bone structure. Mr. Mee believes that the beautiful old cathedral-like church at Hythe is desecrated by the sixpenny peep show within its walls. It is, however, a unique historic monument and 6d or no 6d, its preservation seems to be justified. No one is obliged to visit the place and human bones have often suffered far greater indignities.

[2] i.e. Bankrupt.

Chapter 17

Sin-Eating—More Storms and Floods

1838

JANUARY 1st. Called at Miss Marshall's and she showed me a lovely blue satin gown she has had made for the Charity Ball next Thursday. We called at my uncle John's and asked them all to come to dine next Friday, but Mary says she feels doubtful as Mrs. Henry is no better. Miss Maud called and said they were 'still in the field' but meanwhile her father was very much occupied with the sessions but she asks if Mother would be prepared to add 2 or 3 rooms for the servants and enlarge the coach house. She seems to like the place very much.

January 7th. Sunday. To our delight Mr. Cameron has returned. I received the sacrament and felt very much impressed.

January 8th. There was snow on the ground this morning, but up to now the winter has been mild. I wrote a bit of sad trash for our next Society meeting on having a sanguine temperament. I am sure I wish I possessed one myself.

January 9th. Snowing again and it is lying thick on the ground. Went to my uncle John's and Mary was weeping. Mrs. Henry is not expected to get better. In spite of the weather we had a full meeting, but everyone shivered with cold. Miss Alexander's paper was by far the best and mine was by far the worst.

January 10th. Mr. Lumb advises dearest Mother to do the improvement to suit Mr. Maud. He says it is a wise way to lay out money. I would rather sell the place. Mrs. Swinden called, she told us that poor Mary Scatcherd had been very ill indeed, they feared it might have been St. Vitus's Dance.[1] However, she is much better now.

January 17th. Emma Marshal came to practice duets – Haydn's – and then we walked a little way on the Leeds road but we had to be very careful and walk in the horse tracks. Later it snowed very heavily again.

January 19th. It was so cold in the night that the water in the bedroom jugs and the towels were frozen stiff. The snow is very deep and they say it has not been so cold for 35 years. The ice is falling in small lumps, not round as hail usually is. Our Philharmonic meeting is being put off for a week because of the great cold. The Mauds are to lease Alverthorpe for seven years and Mother will spend 400 pounds at once on improvements. Mr. Cannon is arranging that several of us shall give 6/– a week to help the Polish Jewish family until something definite can be done for them.

January 24th. There was another great fall of snow last night.

January 28th. Sunday. I went to Chapel. The roads were very slippery indeed. Mr. Cameron preached the annual sermon on Death. It was very poetical and learned and I cried heartily about it and about Luther's hymn which always affects me so.

January 29th. Our first Philharmonic concert at the Harrison's which went very well. I played a duet with Emma Marshall and she with Eliza and Playel's first sonata and there was a deal of very good singing. I liked best 'Come let us all a Maying go'. We finished at 9 o'clock and the roads were dreadful; it seemed to be thawing and freezing both at the same time.

February 1st. Jane called. She says my Aunt Wood is determined to leave Wakefield and go to live in the country. We went into town and bought some gloves at the repository and then to the library and got the 'Metropolitan'. Cousin Ann was at home when we returned and she talked a good deal about Mr. Cannon. She says she really thinks Unitarianism is very well for people who are healthy, happy and prosperous but that it is not a religion for those who suffer or are poor and that the ministers are not helpful to such people. She thinks Church Ministers and even Calvanists are better in that respect. I think she just talks this way because she thinks Mr. Cannon is attentive to me. The roads are still very deep in snow but as it is frozen it is not so difficult to walk. This is the fifth week of great cold.

February 3rd. Jane and Eliza and I walked to Flanshaw. The ground is hard and it was quite pleasant. We called at Adam's and ordered wines.

February 4th. Sunday. Mr. Cameron preached on the evidence of a Future State. He told us that in future his two sermons each Sunday will be of two kinds. In the mornings for the cultivated part of the congregation and in the evenings the sermon will be such that even the 'very boys' will understand. I think perhaps I shall enjoy the evening sermon best as I confess I do not always understand him in the morning. When I got home I found dear Mother quite ill and feverish.

February 5th. Dearest Mother is still very poorly. I went to Scott's and bought an aromatic plaster for her that my aunt had recommended. Mr. Cannon called for the subscription for the Jews and he said I should get the Doctor for dear Mother. He said he would call for me tomorrow if I intend to go but I told him that I feared I could not be away from dearest Mother.

February 6th. Dearest Mother is a little better. It is thawing very fast now and the roads are quite impassable.

February 11th. Sunday. Mr. Camerons text was 'Woe unto me if I preach not the gospel' and most people thought that he was preaching at Mr. Cannon and in the evening, instead of a simple talk for 'boys' he gave a long translation from the French on Faith; a most metaphysical thing. I like him very little now.

February 12th. Reading 'The Vicar of Wrexhill' by Mrs. Trollope. It is in ridicule of the Evangelical party and the hero is a monster. It is a disgusting book but so interesting that I cannot put it down.

February 14th. I had to send an apology for not attending our society meeting tonight for I saw that dear Mother did not like me to go. I went for a very short walk with cousin Ann but there was the keenest, coldest wind I have ever felt in my life. The frost still continues.

February 17th. Snow falling very fast. It is my 27th birthday. On looking back and reviewing my conduct during the last year I confess with shame that I have sadly retrograded. I have become indifferent to religion and been worldly and more occupied with temporal affairs. I fear I am addicted to slandering the absent and trying to please the person with whom I happen to be. I dare not say I will never be guilty of these sins in future but do Thou O Lord, help me in time to come to correct all evil and become more devoted to Thee as my years increase. Amen.

February 19th. Mr. Cannon called to see dearest Mother and asked me to go with him to Mr. Morton's lecture tomorrow at the Philosophical Society. He told us that Mr. and Mrs. Burton have heard from their son John who is in America and that he is in sad distress and asking for money to pay his passage back to England.

February 20th. Went to the lecture with Mr. Cannon. Mr. Morton lectured on Geology and Coal which he says is of vegetable origin. It was a very long lecture and Mr. Cameron spoke on the connection between geology and theology and he denied that geology could properly be called a science; rather ignorantly I think, but he was very eloquent as usual.

February 21st. Our Literary Society met at Mrs. Holdsworth's and the subject was 'are animals endowed with reason as well as instinct?'. I did the report of the meeting. We all denied that brutes had reason except cousin Ann and Mr. Cameron. There was much discussion about cruelty to animals – Ann's pet subject. I left at half past eight leaving most of them there. I had toothache and felt ill. It is still very cold. It has lasted now since the 8th of January and has caused much distress to the working people and they say a great number of our songbirds have perished.

March 4th. Sunday. Dear Mother is much better and went to Chapel for the first time for six weeks. She grieved me very much by saying that she would not stay to receive the sacrament. I believe she never would if I did not urge it and her indifference vexes me.

March 5th. I sent a reluctant apology to Mary Ann as I am not well enough to go to our musical meeting today. Mr. Cannon called to ask me to go to the Philosophical meeting again on Tuesday but of course I had to decline, but thought it very kind of him to ask me.

March 9th. Mrs. Lawrance had a baby girl on Friday and she is now very ill indeed. They say she has a consumption. Cousin Henry called and he is very low spirited about Mrs. Henry and seems to think there is no hope at all of her recovery.

March 11th. Sunday. Chapel and Sunday school. Mr. Cameron's sermon was obtuse and difficult to follow. The rent of our pew is to be doubled and dearest Mother is displeased. Mr. Cannon and Cousin Ann drank tea with us. The meeting of Ministers is to be held this year here in Wakefield and Mr. Cannon is busy arranging about it.

March 14th. Miss Marshall called to tell us that Mrs. Lawrance died at nine o'clock but the baby is alive and well. It is very sad as poor Lawrance is left with five children and the oldest not yet 7 years old. Ann called later to ask dearest Mother how to make arrangements for the funeral. Mrs. Lawrance died of consumption and it was very rapid indeed but the baby is healthy. In the afternoon I covered books for the Sunday school.

March 18th. Sunday. Sat with the scholars in the gallery. Mr. Camerons sermon was a continuation of the one last Sunday. I taught Ann's girls as well as my own. Took a walk with Caroline and she told me about the meeting at Lupset which I had missed.

March 19th. The Philharmonic meeting was held at our house. The gems of the evening were 'Here, in a cool grot', and 'The Syren's song'. After the music we danced quadrilles and dearest Mother played for us. Ann was not here of course and I always feel a little lost without her. Mrs. Lawrance was buried by Mr. Cannon on Saturday. They sent me neither gloves nor biscuit.[2]

[1] St. Vitus's Dance was the popular name for a disease called Chorea. It is believed to be a form of rheumatism of the nervous system, characterised by an inflammation of the brain and meninges and sometimes accompanied by damage to the heart, typical of rheumatic fever (Pears med. enc.). It is not a common complaint nowadays, but it assumed epidemic proportions in the 16th, 17th and 18th centuries. A visit to the shrine of St. Vitus was reputed to effect a cure.

[2] The custom of providing gloves for the guests at a wedding or funeral was an ancient one which persisted well into the present century. Black kid gloves of assorted sizes were placed on a hall-table for guests to select their own. Ladies did not attend funerals and so it became customary to send white kid gloves to the female mourners which they wore when attending Church or Chapel to hear the funeral sermon, usually preached within a month of the death. Gloves were originally worn as a mark of respect and token of friendship and peaceful intent. Hostile arms could not be manipulated with gloves on the hands. To draw off and cast down the glove was a challenge to fight. Thus the wearing of gloves at wedding or funeral guaranteed some degree of decorum. The eating of biscuit at wedding or funeral was a custom of very great antiquity, but the practice of sending gloves and biscuit to the absent mourners seems to have become obsolete during the mid-19th century. The question of sending out pieces of wedding cake to the friends of bride and bridegroom is still going strong and no doubt will for ages yet to come. In ancient Rome the Bride's cake played a vital rôle in the wedding ceremony. The Patrician marriage ritual consisted of the breaking of the bride's cake before ten witnesses and no marriage contracted without this procedure could qualify the offspring for holding any High Sacred office. The broken cake or biscuit was then distributed amongst the guests and it was regarded as a talisman ensuring prosperity and fertility. The cake was usually made by the bride-to-be and in Anglo-Saxon days was of the thin scone or biscuit type. The funeral banquet of ancient times much resembled the wedding feast, but its atmosphere and purposes were different. Food was placed in the tomb for the use of the departed in the after world. By eating some of the food set aside for the dead it was believed that some responsibility for his past evil deeds would be transferred to those who ate it. Brewer states that 'sin-eaters' were often hired; some poor creature would accept a coin, a biscuit and a draught of ale and 'so pawn his own soul and let the departed rest in peace'. Gradually this 'sin-eating' ritual lost some of its grimmer implications and the cakes or biscuits were eaten by the guests. A basket of small biscuits was carried round and each mourner took one, and the rest, together with the basket, were then thrown to the poor and often scrambled for in a nearby dusty highway. To obtain a biscuit was considered mighty good luck. The expression 'that takes the biscuit' was not coined yesterday.

Chapter 18

Mr. Cameron Preaches Social Reform

MARCH 25th. My cousins called and talked a deal of nonsense about a certain Mr. T. whom they vow is in love with me. It is so very provoking, for dearest Mother gets so fidgety if she hears my name linked in any way with anyone. Not that she need have the least cause for concern from my part, I just do not know what the foolish girls mean. They say Mary wants Lawrance to bring the children and live with them, but Ann is not very pleased with the idea.

March 26th. Had another bilious attack this morning. After dinner I went with cousin Ann to visit Mrs. Henry. We played with little John for a while and then we went upstairs to Mrs. Henry's room. She wished me to play something on the accordion and I did so, but felt it not the most proper thing to do in the house of a dying person. However, it was her wish. We came away before 6 o'clock.

March 28th. Walked with Mary Ann to Stanley. They are cutting up those beautiful fields for a railroad.

April 1st. Sunday. Mr. Cameron preached a most eloquent sermon but a little rambling and discoursive and I fear I did not benefit greatly. In the evening he continued the same theme which was on the triumphs still to be achieved by Christianity. He said the world is yet in its infancy and our whole social and political institutions are wrong 'so long as a man is not of so much value as a *sheep* we are not truly Christian'[1] and he said a great deal about the state of religion, which did not please my aunt who had gone with us to hear him preach.

April 2nd. Our Philharmonic Society meeting at Julia Harrison's. There was some very good singing, particularly some Italian duets but I felt low spirited and rather poorly.

April 4th. Mr. Cannon came and he had been to Sandal to visit Mrs. Henry. He says she is quite composed and expresses no anxiety except about her children. I went with Ann, Mary was already there. Henry seemed most distressed. Mrs. Henry did not seem to notice that I was there at first, but after a time she spoke to me and asked me to kiss her and again asked me to play for her on the accordion which I did – very reluctantly, then I kissed her again and left her. She seems very weak and to be suffering. It is strange that she should express no fear for her salvation, for if all I hear is true, she has never been a religious person.

April 8th. Sunday. Mr. Cameron lectures to a working men's Association every week now and some of them come to Chapel to hear him preach on Sundays. Today there was a special service for the Association and Dr. Alexander preached and his text was 'The rich and the poor meet together and the Lord is the parent of them all'. After disclaiming all intention of meaning equality of station and circumstances he showed that all men are equal in physical and moral structure and in the sight of the Almighty all were joint heirs of immortality. I thought it a good sermon for the occasion but I know some of the congregation thought it a poor fawning sort of lecture. Mr. Cannon sat in our pew with dearest Mother.

April 10th. Went to my uncle John's. Mrs. Henry died a little before twelve yesterday morning. The funeral is to be on April 14th. I wept with Mary so much that I made my head ache and I went to bed as soon as I got home. Mrs. Scatcherd called and had wine and cake and she asked dearest Mother if any of our Harrogate friends had called (meaning Mr. C. of course).

April 15th. Sunday. We gave our Sunday school scholars a holiday as it is Easter Sunday. It was a very stormy day, but we went to Chapel and were glad we did so, as it was a most excellent sermon. Afterwards Mr. Cannon asked me if I would help him with the boys at the Sunday school; there are many more boys than girls. I said I would but that I could not give up my class of girls for them; I am most attached to them now.

April 23rd. Sunday. Mr. Cannon preached the funeral sermon for Mrs. Henry. It was that very beautiful sermon on the benefits of affliction. I have heard it several times before and it always makes me weep and I felt very serious indeed. In the evening Mr. Cameron read a sermon and not one of his own either. Cousin Ann came home with us and we talked about Mrs. Henry whom Ann tells me was most unwilling to die and only became resigned when she knew it was inevitable.

April 29th. Sunday. Went to Chapel and wore my new bonnet. Mr. Cameron preached on the Ten Commandments. He said that almost all sin is occasioned by our wrong social and political conditions and that if these conditions were not so wrong there would not be so many millions of people without a home or the means of subsistence. He protested that there was great inequality; not even equality of the sexes existed in the world and he said it was the duty of every Christian to pull down the structure of the whole existing Establishment. His language is obscure but there is great danger of his meaning being taken literally. Since he began lecturing to the working men's Association his sermons have introduced more and more about politics and many of our congregation dislike it very much. There is to be the meeting of Ministers here in Wakefield on May 9th. My cousin Ann says she will have nothing to do with it this time. Mr. Cannon is busy organising it.

May 1st. Lord, in Thy mercy, preserve and defend us from all trouble and dangers this month which I always dread. Dearest Mother and I called at my Uncle John's. Lawrance and his four eldest children are now living there. The baby is still at nurse. The three girls are very fine children but the little boy who is a beautiful child is very far gone in a stomach complaint. Dr. Wright was there and he told us that there is no hope of saving his life.[2] Our 'Social' was held at Miss Heald's and everyone was present. Mr. Cameron spoke for most of the time and I thought it dull, desultory and tiresome. Mr. Cannon came away with Ann and me.

May 3rd. Walked with Emma Marshall to Snow Hill Bar and called on old Mrs. Cannon and at my Aunt Wood's, who is very ill. The Philharmonic meeting was held at Marshall's this evening and was quite a merry gathering. I played several accompaniments for them and played a duet with Emma who was less nervous than at our last meeting and then I played 'Liber Augustine'. It was a most agreeable evening. When I came home dearest Mother and I had a long talk about my Uncle John's family and she said she had seen for some time that they were scheming for me to marry Henry. I had seen it too, but I had not acknowledged it even to myself and now I feel very provoked indeed. There is a new law being passed about the marriage of cousins[3] and I hope they will take note of it.

May 9th. A lovely day for the meeting of Ministers and we put on summer clothing and went to Chapel at mid-day. There were fifty people from Leeds, fifteen from Halifax and several from Bradford. Mr. Cameron preached on Death and gave a long dissertation on Dr. Johnson and Spanish writers. After the service we went to the inn and dined. A cold collation followed by tea or coffee. One hundred and forty sat in our room and about one hundred in another dining room. Henry came and sat by me and I thought it very wrong of him to make himself conspicuous so soon after his wife's death and dearest Mother noted that several people observed it. What bitter mortification it caused me! for I know he never did and never would like me except for what I have and I am not so foolish as to be pleased with attention which stems from such a motive. It is all too late now. After dining we gathered in Well's large room and the business of the meeting was dealt with. Mr. Wickstead spoke and many others, but it was not particularly interesting.

May 13th. Sunday. Mr. Cannon asked me if I thought it right to *stand* to sing in Chapel. He said he and the Stansfields wished to do so, and I said I would, so for the first time everyone in the Chapel stood to sing. Mr. Cameron preached another of his political sermons. Amongst other strange things he said that at some future time physical evils would cease and that there would be a day when every little child born into this world would grow up to maturity.

May 15th. Called at my Uncle John's. They were very distressed about one of Ann's cats. Two servants had wished to be quit of it and so had taken it and left it in the fields beyond the old Hall. Ann heard about it next morning and set out at once to search for it. She was quite distracted. Mary sent a servant after her with a pitcher of hot coffee and later went herself to help Ann but they did not find the cat. We think Ann quite insane about animals. Mr. Cannon says she is afflicted with 'catomania' and he told her recently that it is a very morbid and unhealthy feeling which she has and that she should try to rid herself of it.

May 16th. Our Literary Society Meeting was held at Miss Alexander's; besides our members there was a Miss Fisher, an Irish lady, and Mrs. Shepherd. The subject was 'The Sonnet' and each member read a specimen. Miss Alexander read Shakespeare's Sonnet on 'Love' which rather amused us. Several members read Sonnets of their own composition, others read Sonnets by Wordsworth or Coleridge. It was a rather dull meeting. Hannah came for me at half-past-nine and Mr. Cannon insisted on accompanying me too, as he said he did not consider it safe for me to be out with no one but Hannah.

May 17th. Went with dearest Mother to town and ordered a gown and a bonnet – lilac and white, with large French flowers of lilac. Then we went to Barrett's garden and paid our subscription and bought a Camellia Japonica and some roots of pansies.

May 18th. We called to say goodbye to Emma Marshall who is going to London on Thursday to stay for five months. I shall miss her very much. She is going to travel all alone – by a packet, and has promised to write to me four times whilst she is away. I shall be most uneasy until I hear of her safe arrival.

May 24th. Went with dearest Mother to view the alterations at Alverthorpe. We walked around the gardens and across the fields to the Fish pond croft. John Dawson was in the stable yard directing the removal of the last of the carriages. The builders are busy on the new rooms and the Maud family are to move into the house in a few days. We went to my Uncle John's to drink tea. There were several people already there, it was dull and the drawing room was cold but when Mr. Cannon came it was rather better. He talked at length about the Drama which was interesting and then there was a long discussion about Temperance Societies.

[1] A man could be hanged at that time for the theft of a sheep.

[2] This boy, Robert, did not die. He lived to be a spoilt child and a dissipated young man.

[3] Marriage of cousins was much more usual in the past than it is today. The provision of marriage dowries for several daughters could be quite disastrous to the family fortunes. Marriage between cousins prevented the breaking up of estates and kept the wealth in the family.

Chapter 19

Temperance, Drink and Drains

THOSE who preached this new doctrine were dedicated men. They had to be eloquent and they had to be healthy for their lot was foot-slogging over bad roads and sleeping where they might. Those who preached against drink found 'no room at the Inn'. They preached wherever they found listeners – at pit head, factory yard or on open Common land and they were not always welcome. Often they met quite active hostility and the word 'teetotaller' became a term of abuse.

The origin of the word has been much debated; some contend that it was created by a Preston convert with a bad stutter having difficulty with the word 'total' – but that seems less credible than other theories, one being that it was a variation of the spelling of 'tea', the popular beverage of total abstainers. *Punch*, first published in 1841, made merry with cartoons of rough working men and husky Jack Tars delicately sipping tea in transformed bar parlours and asking each other politely 'is your tea quite to your liking?'. A more likely explanation is that it developed from the form of pledge taken by converts to temperance – most of them promised to refrain from beer, wine or spirits for one year except when taken medicinally. To this pledge they affixed their signature or sign, for few of them could write. The more ardent of those reforming, avowed their intention to abstain totally and for all time and so put a capital 'T' for 'total' after their signature. They were the 'T for totallers' which gradually became 'teetotallers'. This new word became established in America very shortly after its coinage in Great Britain and Temperance Societies became a feature of American life in the early eighteen-forties. They paved the way for the Friendly Societies such as the Good Templars and Rechabites which provided medical services and were the forerunners of our National Health Insurance legislation. They were of inestimable benefit to the wage earners, the money saved on drink was spent on better food and better homes. Many poor city workers had little but straw and sacks for bedding and orange boxes for chairs and tables.

However, it would be a mistake to imagine that the new Crusade of Temperance worked a miracle of transformation in the land. Drunkenness continued to be a feature of English life well into the present century. *Delirium Tremens*, now a rare thing, was a disease encountered in all classes and amongst people of all ages and those who died of it were reported as having 'died of natural causes'. Even in the latter part of the 19th century it was considered that to be 'in drink' was an excuse for any offence and not an aggravating factor, as it would be deemed today. J. W. Robertson Scott relates that in the early half of the 19th century, insurance companies sometimes refused to insure the lives of teetotallers or insured them at increased rates. Teetotallers were regarded as 'bad risks'. Today, the reverse opinion is held – but were the companies so wrong at that time? People must drink something, those who drank no beer, wine or spirits had to drink water – dirty water, or perhaps milk (which was dirtier than water) so the view that teetotallers were bad insurance risks was not so odd as it seems to us nowadays when clean drinking water is taken for granted.

In the reign of William IV (1830 to 1837) Sydney Smith wrote: 'Everybody is drunk – the sovereign peoples is in a beastly state.' Samuel Smiles wrote: 'Tavern drinking was carried on by all ranks to a dreadful excess'. People of all ages drank spirits, generally gin or rum; the lowest of the low drank methylated spirits which were cheaper than either of these and laudanum was the final degradation before the pauper's grave. There was a slogan in those days which ran 'Drunk for a penny, dead drunk for twopence'.

However, the drunkenness of all classes at that time should not be judged too harshly or condemned out of hand. There were many causes and it even had a few beneficial effects.

Since the time of the Black Deaths the population of England had doubled. Between 1800 and 1833 it had increased particularly rapidly but sanitation and public hygiene had made no advances at all. Rivers provided the town's water supply and acted as its 'main drain'. Lack of clean drinking water was the chief cause of most epidemic diseases. Drinking of spirits mitigated the evils of the infected water supply. Wine was the chief drink of the well-to-do and it was a healthy beverage. Beer was a safe-ish drink and tea was a real lifesaver as the water for brewing it had to be boiled. Bad as was the situation of the poor due to much drinking of spirits, it would have been immeasurably worse had they been compelled to drink nothing but dirty water. The Beer Houses introduced in 1830 were an attempt to counter the demand for spirits, but for a long time they resulted in further excessive drinking. Had tea been subsidised, and Tea Houses established instead of Beer Houses things might have taken a very much quicker turn for the better. Whisky was not popular south of the border until the 'navvies' popularised it. They called it 'white beer' and found it to be better than rum or gin. Many of the navvies were ex-sailors (hence the name came about – navvies were 'navigators' contracted). Rum had been a ration in the navy and whisky was a new delight. It was, in those days, as colourless as gin or vodka. The colour we now take for granted is an additive.

Borrowing and twisting a phrase of Mr. Macmillan, one-time Prime Minister of Great Britain, it could very truly be said that the rich drank because they had never had it so good and the poor because they had never had it so bad. The Corn Laws and Enclosure Act had enriched the landowners and impoverished the land workers. The homes of the poor town workers were cold, comfortless and insanitary and food was dear. Gin and rum were cheap, Gin Parlours were warm and inviting and as numerous as the stars in the sky on a frosty night. Even children spent their miserably small wages on pennyworths of spirits. The age of children frequenting public houses was between 6 to 16 years. Men earned from 8/- to 12/- a week by working 12 to 16 hours a day for six days a week and women worked equally hard and equally long hours for half that amount and children earned less than half again. Sometimes children began their working life at the age of three or four years; by eight or nine they were 'self-supporting'. Toddlers were given the job of keeping rats away from the workers' food which was generally bread and dripping or bread and cheese, bundled in a red cotton handkerchief. They were also frequently employed in coal mines, opening and shutting ventilators; an easy but monotonous job done in cramped and unhealthy conditions.

Lack of sanitation was perhaps the greatest evil of those days. Privies were of the earth pit type. In industrial areas it was not unusual to find only one servicing from thirty to forty cottages. The better houses had one or two per household, generally situated conveniently close to the dwelling and screened by shrubs and climbing plants such as roses and clematis. The Elder tree was almost always grown nearby as it was reputed to be a fly repellant. These little apartments were often quite convivial places, having one or two 'thrones' for grown-ups and a range of assorted sizes for the younger members of the family. Any amenities other than the actual 'built-in' furniture were left entirely to private enterprise. Buckingham Palace was in no better state than lesser establishments and an open drain ran across the great courtyard. The sewage of all London emptied into the Thames and the smell in hot weather was so overpowering at Westminster that in 1839 there was serious talk of moving the Houses of Parliament beyond the range of the river stench. The joke about 'the smell of the Liffey being one of the sights of Dublin' was a 'joke' which could be twisted to be told of any big town and the bigger the town the bigger the stink.

If there were no nearby river or ditch into which sewage could be channelled, it collected in pits or middens and slowly seeped into the ground, polluting the lower water tables. Middens were rarely cleared, but business firms emptied them on request and sold the 'mixture' as fertiliser to farms and market gardens, and very good fertiliser it was too. Most of the better houses in rural areas had private springs or wells operated by pumps, but these private supplies could become infected by seepage from stable and household middens with quite disastrous results to the householder. Prince Albert, Consort of Queen Victoria, died in 1861 from typhoid, contracted in such a way. Shortly before his death he was making efforts to have the plumbing at Windsor Castle improved. In the year 1853 there were forty-three overflowing cess pits under the Castle. The Prince died before reforms were well under way and after his death the Queen would suffer no further changes to be made. Quite early in the century houses were being 'modernised' by building an annexe or converting a small existing ground-floor room. These 'mod: cons:' were bitterly criticised by many who regarded them as a sign of decadence if not downright wicked and improper – and improper in one sense of the word they must very well have been. It was said that no guest need ever ask or be informed discreetly of its whereabouts – it proclaimed that for itself. Even after the water flush replaced the sand or dried earth flush, this continued to be so, for the waste-pipes leading from the house were untrapped and the problem of sewage disposal was still unsolved. In the year 1880 it was estimated that some quarter of a million of the better houses in London had cess pits below the cellars and the Thames continued to receive the main city sewage. Lord Guildford installed a pump to take the excess odour from his cellar to the open street drain.

It is recorded by John Pudney in his book 'The Smallest Room' that when Queen Victoria visited Cambridge towards the end of the century she stood with the Master of Trinity on the bridge looking down on the Cam, and asked him: 'What are those bits of paper floating down the river?', to which the quick-thinking Professor replied: 'Those Ma'am, are notices, warning the students not to swim'.

Chapter 20

The Years Between

THE journals covering the years between 1838 and 1875 are missing. England had changed considerably in those thirty-seven years. In 1875 Queen Victoria was fifty-five years old and a widow, sad and fat and growing fatter; that is interesting as it demonstrates one of the surprising things about grief – it is not always as emaciating as it is reputed to be.

The Chartists who had disturbed most of the first half of the century had been suppressed by 1842 but their aims and ideals had survived to come to fruition over the years under diverse banners now bearing the composite label of 'British Democracy'.

The famine in Ireland had killed a quarter of the population and driven thousands of Irishmen and women over the seas to America in search of a livelihood where many of them died in misery as great as that from which they had hoped to escape. Things were not quite so bad in England, but the 'hungry forties' and the 'lean fifties' were grim and bitter years, for the workers and their children had a heritage of disease and deformity. Thin gruel made with water or skimmed milk did little for young bones.

The Crimean war had been fought and won and Florence Nightingale had brought a 'new look' to nursing and to the status of women generally. Nurses were no longer just disreputable or drunken types. The Army had its own military hospitals to care for the sick and the wounded, no longer depending on decrepit old soldiers or camp followers. The civilian hospitals benefited by the example of the military reforms and nursing became a respectable occupation for women, though still ranking several degrees lower than that of domestic service.

Oil lamps had superseded candles for domestic lighting and there were gas lamps in the main streets. The lamplighter was a familiar figure at sundown, trudging with his long pole to ignite the lanterns on his beat and reversing the pilgrimage at dawn to extinguish them.

Farming techniques had improved so much that the old wasteful system of slaughtering stock in autumn and salting down meat for winter was no longer in force. There was a changed attitude in regard to such degrading spectacles as public hangings, bull-baiting, cock-fighting and other cruel sports. England was the first country to enact laws for the protection of animals and the first to establish a society for the prevention of cruelty. The Society for the Prevention of Cruelty to Animals led in a curious way to a Society for the Prevention of Cruelty to Children.

In 1865 an S.P.C.A. was started in New York by Mr. Henry Bergh. In the following year a lady came to him for help in the matter of 'a little animal suffering from the unkind treatment of a bad woman'. The case was taken to court successfully and when it was revealed that the 'little animal' was actually a child there was widespread horror and sympathy. There existed at that time no law in any land which gave protection to children. Children were the 'chatels' of their parents and no one had the right to interfere. The public conscience was so disturbed that in the following year a society called the Society for the Prevention of Cruelty to Children was founded. The London Society was established some years later by Lord Shaftesbury – a man who was responsible for many humanitarian reforms, particularly in regard to children.

The Married Woman's Property Act had been passed in 1872 and the 'rights for women' movement was well in its stride but getting little help or sympathy from Queen or Clergy.

In 1875 Trades Unions had been declared legal; until that time all combinations of workmen were accounted seditious. Primary education had become free to the children of the poor in 1870 but it was not compulsory – only about half of them took advantage of the new provision, as wages, however small had greater appeal than literacy.

Since the day when Clara lamented that they were digging up the lovely fields of Stanley to build a railroad, England had been traversed by a network of railways which changed the entire character of the land. In 1839 there were five hundred miles of railway; by 1842 there were five thousand; in 1876 the mileage was as great as it is today.

Medical Officers of Health had been introduced and great efforts made to bring cleaner water to the urban areas. Disraeli's 'Two Worlds' certainly existed but they were not worlds of equal size. For about sixty per cent of the population England was a healthier, wealthier and a happier land. The years between 1845 and 1875 were prosperous years and 1870 was perhaps the peak year, due partly to the Franco-Prussian War, for neutral England benefited, as neutrals usually do. The external trade of the United Kingdom in 1870 exceeded that of France, Germany and Italy put together and was nearly five times that of the United States.

In 1875 Disraeli was for the second time Prime Minister of England – the first and only Jew to occupy that high office and few have occupied it with greater ability or contributed more to England's honour and prestige.

Chapter 21

Convalescence

1875

THE last book is a well conditioned volume, about two inches thick and bound in red morocco. The writing is large and unfaded and almost modern looking. The cipher remains but the long 'S' has gone; it is very easy reading but rather sad and rather dull. Quite two-thirds of the entries are reports of aches and pains, ills and disorders.

August 1st. May God Bless and keep me and if it be right for me, may I live to fill this book. Amen.

My journal was begun when I was fifteen and I am now sixty-four. A paltry record, most people would think, but it has been very useful to me. What to do with all the volumes has been a puzzle to me, I should like them to remain in the family and would rather that cousin Lawrance's girl, Mary, had them than anybody else and hope sometime she might have the patience to read them.

Cousin Ann came to drink tea with me. She is living at Alverthorpe whilst the family are away and spends her time between there and Quebec St. She said very little about the bridal pair. I had a pressing invitation from the Scatcherds to go for a short visit next Thursday and to go with them to the Leeds Exhibition but I wrote to Mary and declined as I do not feel well enough. I took a cab to Lupset and spent the rest of the day with dear Alex.[1]

August 5th. My cousin's girls are visiting at Hatfield Hall so I drove over to invite them all to dine with me next Friday. Mrs. Thomas Barff was there; she told me that she is now seventy-eight. She seemed very glad to see me. At first I did not recognise Nina Wood. It must be 10 or 12 years since we last met, she is quite stout and so very like her poor Aunt Emma. Irene is a tall girl and very plain. They are amiable but have no more style about them than if they had been educated at a Wakefield day school. They showed me Charlotte's wedding photos. They are going on a visit to Queen's Ferry shortly. Tom and Fred have gone back to Greece.

August 7th. A very cold day. There have been very few warm days this summer. I began to embroider collar and cuffs for my new dressing gown. I begin to feel a little more energy now after my long illness and am doing things long left undone. Ashton paid his rents – the last of the Alverthorpe rents! I sometimes wonder if I do right to sell. If Henry pays me promptly and I get the money well and safely invested I shall perhaps not feel so many regrets.

August 8th. Sunday. I dressed for Chapel but the cab did not come and I was less sorry than I should have been as Mr. Barmby I hear, is away and that Mr. Armitage was preaching. I read two of Mr. Charles Beard's sermons which I bought recently. In the afternoon Frank Evelegh called. He is going to lodge in Buxton and go into Manchester to business from there as he thinks it healthier. He is to be married soon to Annie, and hopes they may go to live in London. He says Miss Pilkington's attack was hysterics and that she has fits of it every few weeks and is usually prostrate for 2 or 3 days afterwards. He told me that cousin Henry and the rest are in the Channel Islands and he seems to think none of them will be home for a while yet. He brought me a china milk jug with a cat handle, the cat peeping into the jug. He had been dining with the Briggs. I like Frank very much indeed.

August 9th. Shopping with dear Alex. She has quarrelled with the Barmby's about spiritualism. I bought some bugle trimming and many other things. We saw the carriages returning from the wedding of Kate Wood and Mr. Langhorne and watched a circus drive into town. Then we took a cab back home and spent the rest of the day quietly. We always enjoy being together. There was another thunderstorm in the night. It is a strange summer

– so much rain and the thermometer in the drawing room has never reached more than 62 degrees.

August 13th. Julia Barmby called. Her papa is travelling in Wales – alone, and they think he does not like it and may come home. Poor Annie O'Dwyer is very poorly; fits again. Mr. Stewart (the lawyer) has returned and I must see him. I am becoming anxious about the investing of my money. Cousin Ann called and I asked her when the girls are coming home but she did not say. Mable and Beatrice Barmby and their nurse came with her, but the children were not allowed to eat gooseberries so I gave them some of Charlotte Wood's bride cake to take home.

August 17th. Very hot day; 70 degrees for the first time this summer. I had a letter from dear Alex. Mr. Barmby and Julia called; he did not enjoy Wales very much. Later, Emma helped me to tidy and put away my muslins and laces. It amazes me to see the fine needlework I used to do long ago. Cousin Ann called; she says Henry and Mrs. Henry the 3rd and the two girls are still in the Channel Islands. There was a most peculiar darkness which lasted for a long time this afternoon.

August 22nd. Sunday. A letter from Frank Evelegh. He says all the Clarkson family are about to cross to France. Henry and 'Mrs. Henry the third' will go to Paris but the girls will stay a little longer in Guernsey. He says Mrs. Henry has persuaded Henry to cut off most of his beard. Poor old fellow! Mr. Barmby's prayers and sermon were very good and were over by 11.40, so we had to wait for our carriages. Annie O'Dwyer was at Chapel and seems well, apart from a little hesitation in her speech. Dear Alex was there too. Felt poorly later; I really think the Potass water weakens me.

August 28th. Our Flower Show and Blackburn is busy to and fro with plants from our green house. Cousin Ann tells me that the girls are in France and are crossing alone to Southampton but will not be home for some time yet. I did not go to the Show as I am not able to stand about so I sat on the staircase landing with the children and watched the fireworks, which lasted only half an hour but were very beautiful indeed. Mabel and Beatrice were very good but Beatrice is a nervous child and very frightened by the noise of the rockets. Sometimes I feel that my selling Alverthorpe to Henry is a dream and that I shall never get the money in good investments but I must trust in God and be patient.

August 29th. Sunday. A good sermon but a very wretched congregation. Dear Alex was there. I had a letter from Mary Scatcherd saying her mother is ill. Drank tea at Quebec St. Ann seems to like Alverthorpe Hall better now than she used to do. I suppose it is because it is going to belong to her brother.

September 2nd. Feeling uneasy about the Scatcherds so sent Emma by the railway to Morley to enquire about them. I had a letter from Annie C. They go to St. Malo tomorrow and intend to tour Brittany and Normandy and she says how much they always wanted to do this but how sad to be doing so in such circumstances. I think they make too much fuss about their papa's re-marriage; they have had much enjoyment resulting from it. I only hope that Henry will be back to pay the money and settle everything by October 1st.

September 6th. Cousin Ann called. She walks from Alverthorpe and back twice a day some days and she is 75 years old. Annie O'Dwyer had another fit yesterday. The weather is now very hot. Miss Pollock called to tell me that poor Annie had had eleven epileptic fits since Friday. Making a cap for myself of netting I did forty years ago. It is so fine and beautiful – I wonder how I did it.

September 9th. Went to see poor Annie O'Dwyer and sat half an hour with her. She had not been conscious since Monday morning; now she talked but we could not distinguish what she said and she kept smiling to herself and did not seem to be suffering. Dr. Wright says her right side is quite paralysed and her end is evidently near. I kissed her and took leave and I knew it was goodbye.

September 10th. Dear Annie O'Dwyer died a few minutes before noon and I wept bitterly when I heard. I must put on mourning and think I must buy a black dress, so in the afternoon I went to King and Kingswell's but did not find anything suitable so bought 15 yards of black striped material and arranged for the making of it.

September 11th. Mr. Barmby went to the Registry office and called to ask me to go to the funeral. Several other ladies intend to go, so I agreed. My dress will be ready by then and I think perhaps dear Annie would have liked me to go.

September 12th. Sunday. Chapel and a most excellent sermon but the poorest congregation I ever saw.

September 14th. Dear Annie's funeral was at 12 o'clock and many of her friends were there and a large family circle: Shepherds, Briggs and O'Dwyers. Mr. Walshe's men carried the coffin and there were some beautiful wreaths. The service was that of the Church of England and it was a calm and lovely day – all dear Annies troubles ended and to be with her Heavenly Father, how blest! I brought the children home with me later, they seemed much awed and were very quiet for a while but children quickly forget and very soon became giddy and merry and we had tea in the garden out of dolls' tea things.

September 19th. Chapel and back by cab. A very interesting sermon and some reference to dear Annie. I am not feeling well and I pray may God spare me to get my will made.

September 20th. Had several visitors today and gave them baked ham and chicken and partridges and veal mould etc. Then we played whist. It was pleasant but I was much overtired and did not sleep until after four in the morning.

September 23rd. I lent Emma to the Cromek's to help them with the wedding luncheon. The wedding was at the Catholic Chapel and I went in to watch; they had what they call 'a nuptial mass', of which we could not follow one word. It always seems to me to be awful blasphemy, that talk of turning bread and wine into flesh and blood! The Warringtons were there but no others, apart from the family and the clergy.

September 24th. Alfred Wormold paid his rent for the land he rents at Flanshaw and I told him I must raise the rent. He quite expected it. When hay was 5 pounds a ton he had the land for very little but now it is 9 pounds 10 shillings a ton and the rent should go up. I had a letter from Jane Wood; she says Nina and Irene return to Greece next week.

September 26th. Sunday. That Mr. Robinson preached again; his affectations are intolerable and his voice so low that we cannot hear a word of the prayers. He preached for 40 minutes and it may have been a good sermon had we heard any of it.

September 29th. Henry and his wife came back yesterday. His beard is cut short and he looks the better for it. He is trying to persuade me to take Railway shares as part payment for Alverthorpe. He holds shares in the Lancaster and Carlisle railway which he says are a wonderful investment; best railway in the kingdom and will pay nearly 5%. I told him I did not want shares and do not understand them. My income has always derived from rents. He said in that case, why did I consider a loan to the Wakefield Corporation? But I assured him that the loan would be secured by a mortgage on city property and so it was quite safe. When they left me, dear Alex and Mrs. Hurst called and then cousin Ann, looking very fine in a claret coloured silk gown. She is quite wonderful for her age.

[1] Miss Alexander of Lupset.

Chapter 22

Bulls and Bears, Courts Baron

OCTOBER 1st. Mrs. Henry and the girls called; she was most friendly. I told her I would make my formal call on her next Monday and she pressed me very much to stay and dine with them. I think she does not really like their formal ways and late dinners at Alverthorpe which the girls have introduced.

October 4th. Drove to Alverthorpe to make my formal call. The third bridal call I have paid Henry C.'s wives. I was shown into the drawing room where Mrs. Henry III and the girls were sitting in state. Mrs. Henry was charmingly dressed but wears no head-dress of any kind. I fancied she does not feel absolutely at ease with the girls. The house looked elegant and the gardens very beautiful but I did not feel sad, as I had expected that I might. On the way home I stopped at Goodal's and bought a copy of Tennyson's 'Queen Mary' to give to Mr. Barmby on his next birthday.

October 8th. Mrs Scatcherd and Mary came to dine. Mrs. S. is now quite well and does not look her 85 years. Henry came whilst they were here. He still wants me to take those railway shares and I refused, saying that I do not like or understand shares. He says 'stock' is the right word for railways. I had a letter today from Mr. Cannon who is back in Windermere. Mr. Barmby called and earnestly advised me to have nothing to do with railways. He is more suspicious of them than I am.

October 14th. I had a letter from Helen Wood and she too warns me against shares of any kind. Nina and Irene are now back in Patras. I am reading a novel by Ouida; wonderfully clever and hugely interesting but I feel the writer does not make the best use of her great talents. Today is the 23rd anniversary of the death of my dear Mother and it is just two years since this house was broken into and burgled. I had luncheon today with Mary Warrington and being Friday it was one of their fast days; we had toasted cheese and fish cakes and crabs, a fruit pudding with Porter and wine – they call that a fast! More of a feast than a fast in my opinion.

October 17th. I had a letter today from Lucy Kendal asking me to send her photographs[1] of the Chapel on the Bridge, Mr. Waterton's burial place and one of Walton Hall.

October 18th. I shall be glad when Mr. Stewart's time as Mayor is ended. It makes him so very busy and he has been away every day this week holding 'Courts Barons'[2] and before that he was in London about Waterworks business. It has rained very day this week and I feel poorly and low spirited.

October 24th. Sunday. Not well enough to go to Chapel and I had a quiet service of prayer and thanked God and praised Him and all at once I felt my burdens lifted from me and peace filling my mind and I was happier than I have been for a long time. I know God will help me and guide me. Later, Louisa and Annie C. came with Frank Evelegh and his friend Ralli, a Greek. They had been to church with Mrs. Henry.

November 3rd. Dear Alex and Mrs. Hurst left today for Southport. I am glad I decided against going with them. It is no pleasure to be away from home in such weather as this – cold and wet and dark. Emma is putting up winter curtains and I am embroidering a cover for a footstool. Miss Knight sent a winter mantle for my approval. It is a circular black silk cape lined with squirrel fur and trimmed with velvet. It is very warm and I think I might buy it. It is many years since I bought a winter mantle and I think I can afford it. I have spent very little in the last two years because I was so ill and now I feel quite shabby.

November 11th. I had a letter from Mary Scatcherd, she says they see little of Mrs. Oliver and they are quite horrified and disgusted by her lecturing to the factory women. I went to look at a house which is being built near to the grammar school. It has good rooms, nice marble chimney pieces and it has a *bathroom* and water closet. The worst point is that there are thirteen steps down to the kitchen but as it is on sloping ground it opens on to a tiny garden and is not a cellar, as so many kitchens are. I felt rather attracted by it, but it is a little further from town than this house and might be more work for Emma.

November 18th. Went into town and ordered a dozen bottles of Gilbey's Marsala. It rained, so I took a cab back home and found there a long letter from Mary Scatcherd who advises against the new house I had told her of. Louisa and Annie C. called and sat for an hour and had wine and cake. They say their papa is very sulky lately and they think their new mama is not enjoying her life and complains that Alverthorpe is damp. A case of currants and two boxes of figs and two small boxes of rahatlakoum[3] arrived from Patras and a very nice letter. Mrs. Henry called and brought me beautiful chrysanthemums and Pampas grass.

November 24th. Dear Alex is with me for a few days before going back to Lupset from Southport where she spent three weeks. We went into town and did much shopping and came home in a hansom[4] and dined at three o'clock. Emma went to a Panorama so we waited upon ourselves.

November 25th. It is very cold and much snow on the ground. Henry and Mrs. Henry came and he told me that an oak tree had blown down in the Low Warren onto Deckon's Ings and he wanted to know if it were his or my responsibility. He says he has not yet sold his railway stock as the Bulls and Bears will not look at shares which do not vary in price. I told him I did not know Bulls from Bears but I hoped that he would pay me soon so that I could get my affairs settled. He made no further reference to the oak tree.

November 27th. I read the newspaper to dear Alex. I am grieved to see how her sight fails. I was very poorly all day and rested on the sofa.

November 28th. Sunday. A Mr. Knapton of Bradford preached – he used to be the assistant to George Dawson and imitates him.

November 30th. Snow and very cold. I wrote to Jane Wood thanking her for a hamper containing two pheasants and some pears and walnuts, and many beautiful chrysanthemums. She had written 'carriage paid' on the outside but the railway charged me 3/9.

December 1st. We took a cab and called at the Barmby's. They were preparing a hamper to send to Mr. Cannon and dear Alex and I added several things. Then we went shopping and bought so many things that Emma had to take a clothes basket out to the cab to bring them into the house. We rested most of the day and I felt ill and had the pain in my side again and dear Alex insisted on my having hot flannel to put to my side which I objected to as I know how useless it is. She says I really should call in Dr. Wright again – and I may, but I really believe that the very cold weather affects me. I must begin again to take the Potass medicine.

December 3rd. Thank God, I feel much better today. Dear Alex and I spent a quiet day. I played old music for her, she likes the old music best and we talked over old times and of her love for Mr. Cannon which she has talked of to me often lately, but she has never told me why they did not marry and I and many others used to think they would and neither of them has married anyone else after all these years. I finished some needlework for our Parish Bazaar and cousin Ann called. She seems to like and get on well with Mrs. Henry III.

December 5th. Sunday. Edward (our cab man) came to say that the roads were not safe to drive on because of the snow and ice, so we both read sermons for about an hour and then cousin Lawrance and Mary called and in the evening dear Alex and I talked again of those years when Mr. Cannon was here and of their love affair.

December 6th. Today dear Alex went home to Lupset and we were both sad at parting, God bless her; she is my nearest and dearest friend and she says I am hers too.

December 9th. I had a note from Mr. Stewart telling me of the East Ardsley Gas Co. loan he is arranging for me and they hope to pay 4½% and he says the loan is secured by a mortgage on the Gas Works property. Dear Alex wants me to dine with her on Saturday to meet her nephew Reginald but I have to decline as I feel far from well and the weather is so very cold still. I am reading a book by Trollope – 'The way we live now'. It is full of stories of dishonest lawyers and cheating people out of title deeds and fraudulant speculators – all little calculated to calm me in my present state of anxiety about investments.

December 14th. A note from dear Alex who has had Bronchitis. She says that dear Mr. Gaskell is ill again. Henry and Mrs. H. called; the girls are in Leeds visiting the Miss Marshalls. Henry and Ann seem to have had a quarrel about her rents. Julia Barmby called and invited me to dine with them on Christmas Day.

December 19th. Chapel. A wet and dark day but a good sermon by Mr. B. on the coming season but mostly about berries – the last hymn was a dirge and we all thought poor Mr. Gaskell must have died but it was not so, Thank God.

December 20th. Mr. Barmby sent word to me that our loved and venerated Mr. Gaskell died at one o'clock this morning aged 93. I wrote at once to dear Alex, knowing how much she would feel it. Mary Scatcherd sent Johnson (groom) with a brace of partridges and I sent them a box of currants from Greece. I am busy stitching together the strips of knitting which dear Alex did; 19 of them, and then making a fringe for the resulting sofa blanket. The fringe is 9 yards long.

December 23rd. Mr. Gaskell is to be buried in the vaults of our Chapel on Friday. He wishes for a private funeral, but everybody of any note in town will be there of course.

December 24th. A fine mild day for Mr. Gaskell's funeral. The bells of the Parish Church, muffled, were rung at intervals all the day and such a funeral was never before seen in Wakefield, nor so much real sorrow evinced. I was anxious for Mr. Barmby as it was a most trying service for him. Henry and Mrs. H. called and said Mr. B. had given a beautiful address and every Public body was represented. Henry invited me to dine with them tomorrow but I was very glad to say I was engaged and I also declined his invitation for New Years Day. They had cake and wine.

December 25th. Christmas Day. Cab to Chapel and it was a bright sunny day. A quiet service and very small congregation but better than on previous Christmases but they had decorated the Chapel with evergreens and it looked nice. Julia and Beatrice and Mable had done it, the dear girls. Mr. B. told me he had been invited to hear Mr. Gaskell's Will read and that he had left 1,000 pounds to the Horbury school and 1,000 pounds to our chapel. We played games with the children after dinner. Theirs is a busy house and dear Julia the blessing of it. In the evening we played whist. It was a most pleasant Christmas day and I came home at 9 o'clock.

December 26th. Sunday. Chapel, and the biggest congregation I ever remember in our Chapel. There was a funeral sermon for Mr. Gaskell and 'Vital Spark' was sung most beautifully, chiefly by the Mortimers of Horbury. People of all shades of religion and politics were present.

December 28th. There was a letter today from Emma Kenderdine who has not written since July. She says she is well since she spent a month at Leamington Spa in the summer, but she is having servant trouble – no cook and 'a diseased housemaid' etc. Cousin Ann called and told me a sad story which I could hardly believe. Libby Woolley has left her husband and two children and gone off with a barrister named Grundy. I was so distressed that I could not sleep. Poor pretty little Libby Shepherd who used to be so fond of acting in Charades when we had children's parties here. I know she has been delicate since her marriage and

I have seen little of her. I hear it was not a happy marriage but she must be mad to leave her husband and two little children. I am glad her aunt – (Annie O'Dwyer), has not lived to see this day, the disgrace would have been too much for her and broken her heart.

December 31st. Looking back on the year I feel thankful to God. I am sure my illness was good in many ways; I had so much kindness from people and I lost much of my nervousness and made important decisions such as that of selling Alverthorpe Hall. But since July I have had much anxiety about investments. I have no one to confide in and feel alone. Dear Alex is not that kind of friend and I must trust in God Who has helped me in the past. I think I must remain in this dear old house and not contemplate a removal and I must endeavour to get my Will re-made and my affairs settled and I pray that I may not spend my income selfishly but do a little good with it. So I commend myself to God, asking pardon for the past and help for the future. Amen.

[1] Photography was far from new but in the 1860's and 70's it gained much popularity due to scientific advances which simplified the processes. It was still by no means an amateur's hobby but in the late 19th century Portrait Painters were beginning to gnaw their brush handles.

[2] Courts Baron and Courts Leet are now almost obsolete and were nearly so in 1875. In earlier years they played an important and useful part in local affairs, settling disputes between tenants and land owners and arguments about grazing rights on Common land and many matters affecting the lives of the local people whom they saved from much serious and prolonged litigation. 'Courts Baron' were latterly presided over by the Mayor or agent of the Lord of the Manor and were generally held on rent days.

In 'English Custom and Usage', Christiana Hole writes interestingly of these and other ancient courts held in various parts of England; the strangest of these old courts were perhaps Courts of Pie Powder. They were instituted in the reign of Edward IV and provided for the dispensing of law and order at Wakes and Faires – occasions of great importance in the middle ages. Brewer says that the name 'Pie Powder' comes from the French 'pied poudreux' meaning a vagabond – a tramp – a man with dusty feet. The Courts-pie-powder dealt in a rough and ready way with hawkers and pedlars and such riff-raff of wake gatherings.

It is not beyond the limits of probability that the 'pied piper' was no mesmeric musician but simply a 'pied poudreux' – a vagabond rat-catcher whose angry departure from the district coincided with some local calamity such as a cave subsidence or landslide which engulfed many of the youngsters of the small town of Hameln in 1284.

[3] Rahatlakoum is the name of a Turkish sweetmeat – generally called 'Turkish Delight'.

[4] The hansom-cab was called by Disraeli 'the gondola of London'. It was a light two-wheeled cab, invented by Aloysius Hansom, an architect, of York. The driver sat high up behind the vehicle and communicated with the passengers (not more than two) through a trap door in the roof. There was still one such cab plying for hire in London until about 1920. It was said that it turned out on wet nights only, when theatre-goers were eager for transport of any kind. This type of cab was never used extensively outside of London.

Chapter 23

Income Tax 2d. in the Pound — Trouble in Salt-Pie Alley

1876

JANUARY 1st. I had a long letter today from dear Alex, she tells me that the Mr. Grundy who has gone off with Libby is a married man and that his young wife has just had twins. Mr. Woolley is to sue for a divorce. Emma is not well and says she cannot sleep. Dr. Wright came and ordered chloral syrup and another medicine and said he would come again tomorrow.

January 8th. Very cold and much snow. Emma is better but must continue to take the chloral syrup. I told Dr. Wright about my ailments and he said it was 'just the old kidney trouble'. Mr. Shaw came to collect the income tax[1] which is now down to 2d in the pound. He was not as talkative as he usually is.

February 1st. Visit to Mr. Stewart. He says he can buy preference shares in various gas companies for me which he says 'are much the best for ladies', but he didn't say why. He also proposes a loan on property being developed now near Heath. He says it will give me no anxiety, he will see to everything and I told him that I trust his judgement. I then mentioned my will and asked him if he would act as my executor and he very kindly agreed, so I came home feeling much relieved and thankful to God.

February 10th. Mr. Barmby came and talked about poor Libby. He says she is pining for her children, but Mr. Woolley will not let her see them until she leaves Mr. Grundy. Mr. Barmby says that he feels that if only Mr. G. had taken Libby right away to America, or Australia it would have been better for everyone.

February 14th. I had a Law paper about the Enclosure Act and a printed form telling me to send it to Mr. Marsden. I had one some months ago, but took no notice of it, but this one seems different and perhaps I should ask Mr. Townsend about it.

February 17th. My 65th Birthday. God be thanked for bringing me safely so far on the journey of life. I had several letters and gifts. I spent the morning rearranging my will. I must leave 1,000 pounds to Emma in an annuity and some household effects and legacies to the three Barmby children and to Henry's girls; but to Mary C. I must leave the Flanshaw property as I know Lawrance will not be able to leave her very much. His affairs were so complicated by Robert's extravagant life and by having to pay off his debts when he died. I know poor Lawrance has had to mortgage most of his property but Mary should be very comfortable with the Flanshaw rents and there is coal too which will add to her income some day.

February 19th. Knitting bed socks for our bazaar. Henry came and he asks if I am allowing anything for the repairs he made when he rented Alverthorpe for two years after the Mauds left. I told him very definitely that I had no such intent and that had I sold the place to anybody else I should have got 2,000 pounds more than he has paid me. He little realises that there was a time when he might have had it and much more besides, just for the asking; but that was long ago. He intends to take down the wall between the Warrens to give the grounds a more park-like appearance. He counts too on the fact that there is coal below but I know it might be 20 years or more before those seams are worked, not in his life time perhaps.

March 1st. I sent for a cab and went shopping. Mrs. Henry and her sister called, she is the widow of an Evangelical minister. I gave them wine and cake. They said they think this house is quite delightful and much warmer than Alverthorpe. I pretended to think that they joked but I am sure Mrs. H. is a little vexed; she says that their place is full of birds and she does not like the great dog which goes where ever it likes, into every room in the house, even the drawing room. I think the dog does not like her, for I saw him bare his teeth at her once. She says she has told Henry that if ever his dog bites her she will leave him! Cousin Ann is 76 years old today and I do so wish she would give up all her Anti-cruelty committee work. People still say when they meet 'Has anyone heard any new cat-tales about Ann?' She is so foolish about animals, all the little boys in the town take half drowned kittens to her to get fourpenny bits. They always say they have rescued them from the Beck, where some naughty boys had put them. Then they go off and share the fourpenny bit with the kitten drowners; everyone knows that except Ann.

March 3rd. A letter from Jane Wood. Lieutenant Bird is trying for the post of Chief Constable for the West Riding and they want my support for him but I wrote and told them that I lead such a quiet life now and meet few people; their better approach might be through the Charlesworths. I have no influence now whatsoever. I went to Chapel but felt I got no benefit from it and there was a very small congregation. In the afternoon I helped Emma to plan the garden and wrote to Norwich for seeds.

March 10th. Cab to Chapel and a new driver; I learned that my old driver (Edward) is in a dying state, poor fellow! Mr. Knapton from Bradford preached a good sermon but his train was late and we sat for ½ hour awaiting his arrival. After Chapel I went to see the Bennetts, they live in the Falcon yard. Poor Edward recognised me although he is dying and he said he knew he would never drive me again. He has congestion of the lungs.

March 13th. Mrs. Bennett sent her little grandson to tell me that poor Edward died last night. Dear Alex told me today that the Shepherds are to take a house near London and that Libby will then live in rooms nearby but they cannot allow her to live at home with them because of her little sister Nellie. They hope that 'the sinner' will occupy her days with good works and repentance. It seems they do not think of the pain and suffering she has gone through and her loneliness and pining for her children, they think only of the disgrace of a divorce in their family.

March 14th. Cousin Ann called. She told me that as she passed the top of Salt-pie Alley[2] she saw an Irishman beating his wife and she interfered and he struck her a nasty blow on her arm. All her life Ann has interfered when she saw anyone being cruel to animals and people have always deferred to her but this man frightened her. I really believe it was the first time in her life that she was afraid; perhaps the man was in drink.

March 19th. Sunday. Very cold and thick now, so had a quiet service of prayer at home. I read Mr. Wickstead's farewell lectures with great pleasure. By evening my pain was so bad that Emma put on a mustard plaster for me.

March 28th. Downstairs again after several long days in bed. I wrote many letters and did a little needlework. Julia Barmby called, she says that Sydney Grundy has visited Libby at Bakewell and that he is trying to bring about a reconciliation with Mr. Woolley; all very strange indeed.

March 31st. Went to the China shop and bought a wedding present for Dr. Wright's daughter Nellie. They call it an 'afternoon tea service'. It consists of a china tea tray, small tea-pot, sugar basin, slop basin, cream jug and two cups and saucers and cost one pound, fifteen shillings. I had a cab and called at the Wright's and took it with me and they seemed quite pleased. Mrs. Wright is *very* stout. Called at Quebec St. on my way home. Ann's friend Miss Pelling has just come into a fortune of 10,000 pounds and she is going to buy a clock for our Chapel.

April 7th. The weather has suddenly changed from mid-winter to summer and the days are lovely and sunny and the nights bright moonlight. I packed up all my work for the bazaar, which is to be in Easter week. I have done 3 knitted vests, 3 pincushions, a woollen antimacassar, 3 pairs of bed socks and a knitted cape. I went to bed early feeling tired and poorly.

April 13th. A very cold wind today. We are back in winter again after some lovely spring days. I did some needlework and strove to prepare myself for the Lord's Supper. At 7.35 I had a cab and went to Chapel. There were only about a dozen people there. Mr. Barmby's service was quite beautiful but rather too long.

April 14th. Good Friday and a bitterly cold day.

April 17th. Mrs. Currer Briggs called for me and we drove to Lupset to dine with dear Alex. Mrs. Briggs told me that Oliver Scatcherd and his wife rarely go to Mill Hill Chapel but take long walks on Sunday mornings. Every Sunday afternoon Mrs. Oliver goes to Kirkstall where she has a class of young men for political discussions.

April 19th. Came to Ilkley today. Emma had arranged with old Samson as usual, to look after the garden and the greenhouse and attend to things generally. First class tickets to Ilkley cost only 3/8 each now. We had to change and wait 1½ hours at that dismal little station at Holbeck and change again at Arthington Junction. We arrived in Ilkley just after four o'clock.

May 7th. Sunday. We have been in Ilkley now for 3 weeks and I have not written up my journal as I usually do. Every day is like yesterday, pleasant but quite uneventful. I read and write letters and go for short walks. Emma goes for long walks and brings back handfuls of primroses and blue bells from Middleton Woods. I go to bed early and rest and lead an idle and luxurious life. Ilkley has changed quite astonishingly; so many new buildings and this hillside and the Cow Pasture are the least changed. There are many new Villas but the shopkeepers in the village say that they do not benefit Ilkley as the inhabitants go into Leeds or Bradford to do their shopping. The first Sunday here I went to the Methodist Chapel as it is nearest but did not like it, so the next Sunday I went to St. Margarets and liked the preacher very much. This morning I went to the Independent Church – a beautiful church and I agreed with almost the whole of the service. Emma goes walking with the nursemaid of a family along the road. She looks well and is enjoying being here.

May 15th. Went into the village and did some shopping; mostly gifts and two caps for myself at Miss Turner's. They are made of muslin with high crowns – quite a new style to me – one trimmed with a rose and the other with a lilac flower.

May 17th. Returned to Wakefield and at the station met Henry and the girls. They were setting off to Nostell. I went by cab to the Barmby's whilst Emma went to open up and prepare the house for me. The Barmbys were all glad to see me and I them. I took Mable a writing case for her birthday; she was 11 last week, and a smaller one for Beatrice and gloves for Julia. I went home after dinner and Emma had fires burning and everything looking as if we had never been away.

May 20th. Mr. and Mrs. Hancock (from Patras) called. They and five of their children are visiting at Hatfield Hall. They say that Lieutenant Bird is there too. He does not intend to remain in the R.N. and is very anxious to get this post as Chief Constable of the West Riding, but things like this might be easier to arrange in Greece. In the West Riding there are four hundred magistrates whose votes he will need. When they left I walked along to Bennett's to arrange about my cab. Poor Edwards son is to drive me in future.

[1] When Peel introduced income tax it was at first sevenpence in the pound and later reduced to fivepence; in 1876 and 1877 it was reduced to twopence. Since those two memorable years it has risen steadily and the trend nowadays seems to be for the government to take the pound and hand the twopence back to the tax payer.

[2] Salt-pie alley is a name of the same vintage as 'Courts of pie-powder'; 'Pied-sale' were even of less repute than were 'pied-poudreux'. Salt-pie Alley was a mean little by-way of slum dwellings. Irish labourers were easily distinguished from the local poor by their style of dress – they generally wore ragged velvet tail-coats, brightly coloured vests and battered, once-white, beaver hats. They worked hard for very low wages but spent most of their earnings on Scotch whisky.

Chapter 24

Getting a Will Signed and Investments Arranged

MAY 21st. Sunday. Chapel. Mrs. Archie Briggs was there and Mrs. Marriot and both in better health. It was good to be back in my own pew again. Mr. Barmby preached a good sermon. I feel much improved in both health and spirits by my visit to Ilkley, thank God for it. I went into the Barmby's after service to see dear little Beatrice who was on the sofa in one of her feverish attacks.

June 1st. Thank God May[1] is happily over. I always dread it. I had on my bonnet and all ready to go out walking when Emma announced 'a gentleman from Mr. Stewarts'. It was Mr. Stewart's managing clerk; Mr. Stewart being himself ill in bed. He gave me a draft of my will to look over and check and a list of the investments Mr. S. has arranged for me. Mr. Barmby and Ada made a long call, they are going to London next week and will call on my cousins at Guildford. Samson has been busy in the garden and Blackburn too and Emma planted out geraniums.

June 11th. Sunday. A Mr. Robinson preached and a most disagreeable and tedious person he is. The sermon lasted ¾ of an hour! Afterwards I went in to see dear Beatrice who has been ill and Dr. Maffey thinks very poorly of her state. The dear child (aged 8) was reading with great enjoyment 'The Lord of the Isles'. I stayed and played the piano for her and then Mable, Julia and Bee and I played besique. I left at 9 o'clock. The weather is very beautiful and the Laburnum and Pink Thorn have been better this year than ever I saw them.

June 12th. Walking in the garden and find we have not one gooseberry in consequence of old Samson cutting them so badly in the winter. Annie and Louisa called, they tell me they are going with Edith Guest on a six weeks tour of Ireland. Mrs. Hurst called, she has been in Harrogate with dear Alex; whilst there she bought a table and a walnut Davenport and Alex bought one too. They gave five pounds for the Davenports. I had a long letter from Mr. Cannon, mostly about the election of a Mr. Hargrove as Minister at Mill Hill Chapel (Leeds). He was a Dominican priest four years ago.

June 22nd. Weather very hot and I am feeling poorly. Mr. Stewart is in London again on Waterworks business. I feel some slight misgiving about one of the investments he has arranged for me at $4\frac{3}{4}\%$ interest. It seems there might be some element of risk in so large a rate of interest, but I must trust in God and try not to be too occupied by wordly affairs.

June 29th. Went to town and bought gloves and a scrap book for dear little Beatrice. She and Julia and Mable came to tea with me. Mable is quite a tall girl and most affectionate. She amused herself by helping Emma to weed the garden. Julia says that Dr. Maffey says that her bad throat was caused by the gas tar now used in our roads. When they left I made a cap for myself out of yellow lace which is very fashionable now – given to me by dear Alex.

July 1st. Had a letter from Edith Higginson to tell me that her father has become suddenly worse and must give up preaching at once. He is suffering from valvular disease of the heart. I played the piano in the twilight as I often do. It brings back old scenes, but not unhappy ones, thank God.

July 6th. Emma is making rhubarb wine. Mr. Wagstaffe came, bringing another man to witness my signature to a deed of conveyance for Alverthorpe Hall and the mortgage deed of the E. Ardsley Gas Co. so that it can be registered. The man Mr. W. brought did not utter one word but just stood by, holding a piece of blotting paper in his hand. When they left I felt sad, thinking that I had parted with the old place forever, but it was never happy for me so I should really not be sad.

July 14th. Went shopping and I met Mr. Whitaker who told me that the whole Woolley-Grundy divorce case is reported in the Leeds Mercury;[2] all the most piteous letters and private matters made public. Today the heat is tremendous – too hot for any kind of exertion and sleep is not easy these hot nights. I am very glad the Barmby's are all away at Yoxford and will not see the local papers about their cousin's affairs.

July 16th. Chapel and a most excellent sermon from Mr. Squire on the 'Unknown God'. Everyone complained of the heat. It is hotter than it has been for many years. I went to bed early feeling ill, feverish sickness and pain – perhaps it is due to the great heat.

July 28th. Emma went for Dr. Wright. He says it is just 'the old trouble' and gave me a box of very nasty-smelling pills.

August 2nd. I had a long interesting letter from Louisa C. written from some place in County Donegal. The girls are enjoying their tour immensely and are to be away two more weeks. Dr. Wright came and seemed surprised to find that I am still far from well. He gave me a prescription to take when the pain is bad – chloroform and laudanum. Later, dear Alex's nephew Reginald called. He is staying a few days at Lupset and he questioned me about my ailments which I quite resented, but he meant it kindly. I showed him Dr. Wrights prescription and he said 'no doctor in England could do better'. I do wish dear Alex would not talk to him, or to anyone, about my health.

August 5th. Dr. Wright came again and seemed concerned to hear of my having so much pain, and said I must take the potass medicine 3 times a day. Dear Alex came and is pressing me to go to Harrogate with her but I do not like Harrogate now. She brought me several books to read and was most kind. I had a letter from dear Julia Barmby; they have been twice to the Crystal Palace and to the British Museum and the Royal Academy.

August 9th. Dr. Wright came and said I must continue with the same medicine. He talked a lot about his son Fred who has just returned from his 2nd visit to China and is very ill. The hot weather continues and Dr. Wright thinks it might be the cause of some of our troubles.

August 13th. Sunday. Chapel in spite of feeling very weak, but the Barmby's are home again and I wanted to welcome them. I hear that last week there were only 12 people at Chapel but today we had a tolerably good congregation. Mr. Barmby preached a good sermon and I was glad I had gone. I cannot do without public worship. The heat was excessive and I spent the rest of the day on the sofa. I do not remember ever having so long a period of great heat.

August 14th. Mr. Barmby called and gave me all the news of the Woods and the Shepherds. The temperature rose to 104° and everyone is feeling exhausted. Mrs. H. III called, she told me that Henry is summonsing some boys for bathing in his fields on Sunday morning. I told her that had been done ever since I remembered and I don't think Henry can stop it; she had tried to get the boys off.

August 18th. Dr. Wright called but talked mostly about his son Fred who is very ill – 'matter forming between the inner ear and the brain'. Dear Julia called and we sat in a shady spot in the garden. It is so very hot but in the evening there was a very welcome shower.

August 22nd. Dr. Wright came and I asked at once about Fred. He said 'Oh Miss Clarkson, I am crushed' and indeed he seemed so. Fred had an operation on Sunday; a hole made in his skull, but it has done no good and there seems to be no hope whatever for him. He did not order any change for me and I really did not like to talk of my ailment when he is in such great trouble himself about Fred. The Sunday school feast is being held today at Sandal Grange but I was not well enough to go. I wrote to Ilkley about rooms for myself and dear Alex and Miss Lamport.

August 26th. Dear Alex sent me a pair of grouse. Several people called after visiting the Flower Show. Henry and

Mrs. H. and the girls looking brown and coarse after their Irish tour. They should guard their complexions better! Julia and Mable and Beatrice came after five and we watched the fireworks together at dusk.

August 27th. Sunday. Chapel and Mr. and Mrs. Archibald Briggs took leave of us all; they are leaving Stanley Hall and this district for good. An uncle of Mr. B's has left him a cork forest in Pernambuco and they think living in a warmer climate will be a help to Mrs. Briggs who has a consumptive tendency.

August 30th. I was glad that Dr. Wright called and he told me to discontinue the Potass water. Both his sons are very very ill. Fred is no better for the head operation and Edward has bleeding of the lungs.

September 1st. Dr. Wright came again today. He thinks there is some obstruction or irritation of the lower bowel which causes much of my pain and he advised castor oil each morning. Both his sons are still very ill indeed. I wrote to Mr. Stewart and told him I go to Ilkley on the 12th and would like to get my will fixed before then; life is so uncertain and my health is so broken, I shall have an easier mind when it is done.

September 2nd. Mr. Barmby came with the children and Louisa C. was here too. He hinted that they might leave Wakefield in the near future but it was only a hint. Still, I do know he has engaged a preacher for Ossett and Barnsley at 50 pounds a year and I believe he might go if he found some other place. He told me that the Iron Works of the Briggs' at Middlesbro' have not paid a farthing to the shareholders and it is rumoured they are about to fail and that would be sad; some of his wife's money is in it I know – all the O'Dwyers had money in it.

September 5th. I had a cab and did some shopping and just as I arrived home Mr. Wagstaffe arrived about my will. Mr. Stewart is still very ill and confined to bed. I gave him the copy I had written out and explained that I wished Emma to have 1,000 pounds in an annuity and furniture and my wearing and household linen. We talked for a long time and he had cake and wine. I like him, but there are stories of his flirting with pretty maid servants. He comes from London and has some kind of degree and is quite gentlemanly. He is Mr. Stewart's managing clerk and does much of his confidential work.

September 7th. Mr. Wagstaffe came, bringing with him the same silent man who had witnessed my signature before. I looked carefully over the will before signing and pointed out that one or two names were mis-spelt, but it seemed all quite correct otherwise, so I signed on every page as he did and so did the silent man. Mr. Wagstaffe took the signed will back to Mr. Stewart's office and it is to be kept in his will box. And so it is done and may God prosper it. Amen. When they left Dr. Wright came. He says poor Fred is very near his end. Walter has been to the ship and brought away all his belongings. Poor Edward is very ill too and has had another lung bleeding.

September 8th. Went to see Samson (gardener) who is very ill, poor fellow. I gave his daughter 5/– for brandy for him. Mrs. Scatcherd and Mary called and brought me a pair of partridges.

September 12th. Sent Emma to enquire about old Samson and take some money for brandy. Then we locked the house and set off at one o'clock. At Westgate station we met dear Alex with her maid Margaret and Miss Lamport who is taking her cook. We had to wait an hour at Holbeck and got to Ilkley at about four.

September 17th. Sunday. We did not go to a place of worship. Miss Lamport read to us from a lately published volume of sermons of Mr. Cameron's which I recognised by their style almost at once. She read beautifully! Then we had some hymns and religious conversation, so we did not spend our day ill. Miss Lamport is an invalid from a spinal complaint and she uses an India-rubber air cushion and hot water bottle and many other things to help her comfort. The servants are happy together. Miss Lamport's cook is the same age as Emma and she and Margaret go out together for long walks on the Moors.

[1] Clara's dread of the month of May was perhaps a relic of an ancient superstition. The Romans thought it unlucky to marry in May. In this month the women held the festival of Bona Dea, the goddess of chastity and in May too was held the feast of the dead – the Lemuralia. The early Christians did something to dispel this prejudice by dedicating the month to the Virgin Mary. The names 'Mary' and 'May' have no connection in origin.

[2] Freedom of the press nowadays does not include freedom to report details of Divorce Court proceedings.

Chapter 25

Typhoid Outbreak – 'Rights for Women' and Rain Water

OCTOBER 10th. Back to Wakefield and Emma soon had everything comfortable. Mrs. Hurst called and Lucy Micklethwaite. She says her sister is ill of typhoid fever; their cook has died of it and a housemaid very ill of it and the groom also. Mrs. Henry came and she says Henry has been dangerously ill and he says he may not live long, so she told him that he must face things and prepare to meet his Maker!

October 16th. Letter from Emma Kenderdine. They are making their drawing room into a billiard room and she has now better servants and seems happier. She says Libby Shepherd has disappeared from her lodgings and Mr. O'Dwyer and Mrs. Shepherd are suffering great anxiety and do not know where she has gone, but we all can guess. I drove to Woodhead's colliery and paid for a year's coal. I asked him when he would be likely to want my coal. He said he only wished that he might want it, but that there is little likelihood at present. I came back by town and bought scarlet and black striped flannel for a nightingale.[1]

October 20th. Mrs. Hurst called and told me that poor young Dr. Fred Wright died last night. Edward is very weak and ill. Mrs. Henry called to take leave; she is going away for several weeks. She told me that Captain Evelegh has lost his appointment at Portsmouth. There are many reasons given but most people say it is all his father-in-law's fault but Annie C. says it is his wife's cousin's fault – Mr. Bonham Carter, who wants the place for his own son. It is very sad for Mrs. E. they will have to give up their house to this young fellow and it is the house she was born in.

October 23rd. Very ill in the night. Bore it as long as I could but at 2 o'clock rang for Emma who got me hot bran bags and made some tea. I did not get up until very late. Julia and Beatrice called and then Mrs. Sidebottom with her servant, she, so smelling of gin, I could scarcely bear to be near her. Later Mrs. Micklethwaite came and Emma went to Brook's for her, for the register of her poor cook's death. Ada is recovering slowly from the fever. I spent the evening making my nightingale.

October 30th. Took my ivory locket which dear Alex gave me to have a likeness of my dearest mother put in it at Mr. Hall's. He told me of the sad death of Cardwell's wife, killed by falling down the station steps. She was only 34 but has been given to drinking habits for two or three years. I went then to Ainley's taking a small water colour drawing by Mr. Cromek which the girls gave to me. He did it at Ostia in Italy in 1832, also two chromo-lithographs of Bolton and Kirkstall Abbeys to have them framed. On the way home bought a hare (5/–) at Pollard's.

November 1st. Mr. Barmby called, he wanted to take me to vote at the municipal election which I declined to do. I went for a walk along the roads, now no longer lanes. There are buildings all along Pindar Fields and quite close to here on every vacant space. After dinner Mrs. Oliver Scatcherd called, she is engaged in this 'female sufferage' cause and addresses factory women and others on Political Economy. She has given up public worship altogether and is as far advanced as any of these foolish women we read about. She talks of her talents (and she is clever), and she boasts of her acquaintance with Professors and such people. Louisa and Annie C. came in when we were drinking tea and she set forth one of her pet theories – that nobody ought to have children except those who can afford to keep them themselves. 'People say God sends children! He does nothing of the kind.' She says the C. of E. marriage ceremony is disgusting from beginning to end. When she left I was so exhausted I could not sleep all night, she was like a whirlwind and I became too excited.

November 4th. We have now a new gardener. He charges 3/6 a day and Emma gives him drinkings of beer, and bread and cheese and coffee. She says he works well.

November 6th. Miss Pollock called and a man came for the Poor Rate and the Urban Sanitary Rate. Louisa and Annie C. came and soon after they arrived Mrs. Oliver Scatcherd arrived too. She harangued us on her favourite topics and it greatly amused Louisa and Annie. I must give her credit for being thoroughly earnest. I should not like to live with her and I don't think she is interested in anything but her one topic. Poor Samson's daughter called to ask me to write to Mrs. Wheatley Balme about her father. She felt sure they would help them if they knew he was in want. I gave her 2/– and half a bottle of brandy for him. It was snowing heavily today. I went to bed early having much pain and bouts of shivering. I sent Emma to pay a bill for me at H's. She says he was very drunk but gave her a proper receipt.

November 8th. Did some shopping and when I came home found Mr. and Mrs. Barmby there. Mr. Barmby told me that he and Beatrice and Mr. Naylor were walking to Lupset a few days ago when Mrs. X. overtook them in her cab and insisted on their getting in and she drove them to Miss Alexander's. Poor Mrs. X. drinks sadly and Mr. B. did not like being seen with her, but she meant it kindly so they had to accept. I sent Emma to pay Dr. Wright's bill which was much smaller than I had expected for 12 months and he gave Emma 2/6 for herself. I fear I am beginning to have another cold. Annie C. came to borrow a Greek dress for a fancy ball. They have several guests at Alverthorpe for the Bachelors' ball and this fancy ball.

November 10th. I am now giving Emma 16 pounds[2] a year. I do hope she will be sensible and save. She is a good kind girl and I feel that she deserves this increase.

November 11th. Cousin Ann came; really for a subscription for her Anti-cruelty Society. It is high time she gave it up and many other things too. I had a long letter from Jane Wood. Captain Edwards and Charlotte are now back in

Patras as he has no ship at present. Mrs. Barff Charlesworth and Mrs. Nicols made a long call. I had not seen Mrs. Nicols for three years and she is very stout now. They came in a fine open carriage with a pair of fine horses and two liveried servants.

November 12th. Not well enough to go to Chapel so read Dr. Farrar's 'Life of Christ' which I like very much. I had a letter from Emma Kenderdine. She tells me that she went to one of those women's sufferage meetings on purpose to see Mrs. Oliver Scatcherd and was introduced to her.

November 15th. Emma went for Dr. Wright and we talked about my symptoms. He said the pain is caused by the stones. He said that pump water might not be good for me and that I had better drink Apollinaris water for a while instead. He talked much of poor Fred. Mrs. Scatcherd and Mary called and stayed to dine with me. They talked of Mrs. Oliver and her strange ideas and about her telling working women not to have children and they say it is quite untrue about her being a 'total abstainer'.

November 18th. Dr. Wright came. He says he is not quite content about my having Apollinaris water but that I had better not drink pump water. He wants me to drink only rain water. Miss Pickard called and I lent her one of Dicken's novels. I played the piano at dusk as I now do so often and get great pleasure from it.

November 19th. Sunday. Chapel – Mr. Barmby preached on 'self conceit' and he took the opportunity to point out that the end of Mark's Gospel as well as the beginning of Luke's were *not* authentic. I am grieved that he should say such things. I had a letter from the Higginsons. His presentation was 600 guineas and a silver inkstand. I had a letter too from Helen Wood who says that their house was flooded and they have had to have floors taken up, with streams of water running below like rivers and their drains will have to be re-laid.

November 20th. Emma went to Mr. Crowther (dentist) to have a tooth stuffed. When she came home she told me that Mrs. X. died last night. The poor thing was a sad drinker and has been the towns talk for a long time. Her husband took her from home all summer, travelling around, but when she came home she was no better. They say she used to get the wife of her cab driver to get the spirits for her and they used to drink together. She was found dead in the house of the cab driver, lying on a bed by the drunken wife. She was 47 and there have been several similar cases in Wakefield recently.

November 21st. Mrs. Micklethwaite called to take me to Lupset to visit dear Alex. Mrs. M. now drives a small open one-horse carriage called 'a Victoria' and it is very comfortable. I was well wrapped up and enjoyed the drive.

November 22nd. I had a letter from Patras. Tom says that if there is not a war he intends to come over to England this next year. Louisa came and told me she has had an offer from a young Irishman whom she met in the Isle of Achill. He had given her a seal skin and taken her out several times in his yacht. He has never lived anywhere else but on the West Coast of Ireland and never intends to live elsewhere; he has an estate there. But I do hope Louisa will not accept his offer. She could never be happy living in such a dreary, lonely, far away spot.

November 24th. The Chrysanthemum show, but not well enough to go. I sent Emma and she called at Carpenter's and ordered Sherry and Marsala. The first stone was laid today of the Clayton Hospital by Mr. Charlesworth. There was a procession and Masonic honours, but the rain was quite dreadful.

November 27th. Dr. Wright came. He altered my prescription and we talked for a long time about his son Fred. He is copying his diary and says that Fred was 'his younger self'. I sometimes have just a doubt that dear Alex may be right and that Dr. Wright does not quite understand my case. She wants me to consult her nephew Reginald but I have had Dr. Wright for 35 years and feel reluctant to change to so young a man. All my friends urge me to have further advice. I had a letter from E. Kenderdine, she says her hair is quite 'mouse' now and very thin, but skilful millinery saves her from having to wear sham hair. I had a letter too from Mrs. W. Balme enclosing five pounds which she asks me to give to poor Samson and she asks me to let her know how the poor fellow is.

December 2nd. I drink filtered rain water now. Louisa and Annie came and they say that nowadays an operation can be performed for stones and entreated me to see a Dr. Lloyd of Harrogate. I felt quite sick with horror at the thought.

December 4th. Mr. Wright came and we talked a long time about the Gaskells. Charles is to be married this week to Lady Catherine Wallop. At last he said, 'I must not sit here gossiping – how are you?' Later Mr. Barmby called bringing that Mr. Naylor with him whom he has lately engaged for his mission services at Ossett and Barnsley. He is to give him 50 pounds a year. He has a wife and two children and comes from Weston-super-Mare where his wife keeps a school. He is about 50 and is a most silent man, but he *can* talk and seems to know something about many things, but I feel that he is most unsuitable for Ossett or Barnsley – his opinions are *very* advanced indeed.

December 8th. Dear Alex called with her nephew Reginald who was most anxious that I should have morphia injected when my pains become very bad. He showed me a little instrument and how to use it and said I should suggest it to Dr. Wright – as if I would dare to do so! Everyone gives me advice on my diet and if I took notice of everyone of them I would be living on rain water and dry bread.

December 11th. Dear Julia, Mable and Beatrice came to tea. The two children were so good and quiet and played card games and they are good at them, as all the Shepherds are. Mable will not eat meat now because she thinks it is wrong to kill animals. She will grow up to be like cousin Ann! I had a letter from Jane Wood telling me about their nephew Harry who is now married and living in Varna and has three children. He hopes there will soon be a war 'for the good of trade' and says we should not believe about the Bulgarian atrocities.[3] He says the

Christians in Turkey are a most degenerate set; Mohammedans infinitely superior. He asked her to send out to him his poor mother's jewellery. A hamper of currants and figs arrived today from Patras. A letter too from Annie C. who is visiting at Wood Hall near Harrow.

December 20th. Heavy rain and floods in many places. Sent Emma to visit old Samson and take him a cake and 5/–. Spent much time directing Christmas cards and writing letters.

December 24th. Sunday. Very cold and much snow. My driver came to ask if I intended to go to Chapel but I said no and was glad I had done so as a horse fell in the shafts close by here. The Scatcherd's groom came yesterday with a quantity of grapes and a cake and I sent figs and currants to them.

Christmas Day. There were bands of music and singers in the night. It was a fine morning with thick snow on the ground and later it snowed again. I had a cab to chapel which the dear girls had decorated beautifully. Mr. Barmby read the 1st Chapter of Luke – not one word of it which he believes, as he told us afterwards. I told him I thought it was a pity he should read it in Chapel. There was a very good sermon and we sang the old tune of 'Christians Awake' to some words printed on a card. A small congregation but as good as could be expected for Christmas Day. I spent the day at the Barmby's. Mr. Naylor, the Missionary, his wife and two daughters were there too. After dinner we gathered around the Christmas tree and exchanged a great number of gifts. Later, we played whist and I came home at 9 o'clock.

December 26th. I had a 7 page letter from Mr. Cannon who is now 86 and a letter too from dear Alex. There is very heavy snow. Dr. Wright came and seemed quite surprised to hear how free from pain I had been for two weeks. He said, 'No doubt due to the rainwater' but I said I could not be sure of that until a much longer trial had been given. Part of our garden wall has fallen down as a result of the great amount of rain we have had recently.

December 30th. Spent much time this morning doing my accounts. I notice that everything is about twice the price that it was ten years ago.

December 31st. Sunday. Chapel and a most excellent sermon from Mr. Barmby; the annual one on Death, Judgment and Eternity. 1876 is almost gone and I thank God for His great mercies to me. I have got my will made and my affairs settled and have now a better income than I have had for several years. My health has been bad and I know I have a fatal disease but I am truly thankful to God that I am now having much less pain. May God give me the grace to do His will. Amen.

The last surviving journal ends on this pious note, but in spite of the 'fatal disease' Clara lived to fill several more volumes. She died on the 9th of October 1889 at the age of seventy-eight.

[1] This garment was probably an invalid bed wrap or jacket called after Florence Nightingale.

[2] By present standards this seems an incredibly small wage, but was at that time quite a good one. Housemaids were paid 10 to 12 pounds a year and a good cook 20 to 22 pounds. A governess was thought to be handsomely paid at 30 to 35 pounds a year. Domestic servants generally slept in attic bedrooms and worked in cellar kitchens. They were on duty or on call 24 hours a day, had one evening off each week and a half day holiday each month. Nevertheless they were immeasurably better off than those who worked in factory or mill. They had good food, healthy surroundings and good clothes provided by their employers. They were looked after when sick and usually provided for in old age after long service in the one family.

[3] The Bulgarian atrocities had been in the news for many a long year but it was not until 1878 that the Russians marched into Bulgaria to rescue Christians from Turkish misrule. There was great sympathy in England for the sufferings of the Christians in the Balkans, but the balance of power in Europe was delicately poised and the possible Russian threat to the Suez Canal was not to be tolerated, so England resounded to the song:

'We don't want to fight
But by Jingo if we do
We've got the men, we've got the ships,
We've got the money too!
The Russians shall not have Constantinople.'